from Bec To Hannah

My pen is my harp and my lyre
My library is my garden and my orchard

Dedicated to
Ciaran Finnbar Walton
Whose heritage this is

A Harp of Fishbones

Russell Walton

The White Row Press

A Harp of Fishbones

Russell Walton

The White Row Press

First published 1992 by
the White Row Press
135 Cumberland Road, Dundonald
Belfast BT16 OBB

Cover illustration: Ian McCullough
Text illustration: Geoffery Fulton

Typesetting by Island Publications
Printed by The Guernsey Press Company Ltd

A catalogue record for this book is available
from the British Library

ISBN 1 870132 60 2

Contents

Preface

The popularity of the harp has increased beyond belief in the last thirty years, since it first began, in the late fifties, to interest me as an instrument. Today we have legions of instruments, makers, teachers and composers, many books and tutors have been written, and the number of recordings of harp music is now quite voluminous.

This is all very fine, but up till now we have had little in the way of books about the harp in history, in legend or in folk tales. I now have the pleasure of introducing this delightful and very charming volume of harp stories in legends, fairy tales and folk tales, from around the world, by Mr Russell Walton.

It will immediately strike the reader that, at one time, the power of music was credited with the ability to heal, to cast a spell, to have a very real effect on human life, and to invoke the power and support of invisible beings, such as the various nature spirits, angels and Gods!

The music of the great masters also has these powers, but Western civilisation has failed to make a study of the effects of folk music, popular song, or the music of the inspired classical masters. Few realise that the music of Handel inspires dignity, religious devotion, and also has had an influence on human manners, or that the music of J. S. Bach develops the intellect, also inspires religious devotion, and that it provided the inspiration for the German philosophers of the late 19th and early 20th century, whereas the music of Beethoven portrays the deep layers of the subconscious mind, and expresses sympathy with the prostitute and the prisoner as in Fidelio, while the music of Schumann portrays the child's mind, and that of Frederick Chopin portrays the aspirations of the aristocracy, had an effect on the emancipation of women, and, like the music of Handel, increases the refinement of human manners.

It fails to occur to most people, musicians included, that each great Western composer's music has had a very definite effect on humanity at large, and that the composer in question was not just working for the good of his health! The spiritual hierarchy of our planet chose these masters to write very definite forms of music for various aspects of human development.

Music has always been the most occult of all the arts because it "begins where words leave off", and has an absolutely immediate effect on the listener. We have quite failed to carefully and scientifically study these effects, but this does not reduce them. Any law is true and does not depend on our belief. Truth does not ask for our opinion.

We now live in an age where the spiritual hierarchy secretly encourages the spread of the ethnic folk music of all countries, because the time has now come for all countries to learn to work with one another in true synarchy. Instead of one country asserting its supremacy over all others, now that country must ask itself, "How can this country contribute to the good of all other countries?" No country is superior to another, but each country has something unique which it may contribute to the whole world. The higher powers are now inspiring a new interest in ethnic music, art, poetry, and folk tales, so that such a universal attitude will be encouraged amongst us all! Therefore, this excellent book has timely and timeless importance.

Harpers will love these stories, but this is not just a collection for connoisseurs, it will delight all kinds of readers and touch anyone who has a feeling for music.

Harpers will perhaps especially enjoy the anecdotes about such men as Denis Hempson and Turlough O'Carolan, but many stories such as "The Living Harp" are deeply instructive when one understands the mystical and symbolic meanings hidden behind them.

Music still possesses the power referred to in these stories. Any series of notes can be played in a certain way and one may feel sorrow or pain, or perhaps a healing or love vibration, but the particular instrument that is played will also have an effect. The organ, the harp, and the flute, have a very spiritual effect, and strings and woodwind can affect the emotions or mind, but brass instruments and percussion affect us in our physical bodies. A lot depends also on the character of the music played, so that muffled or muted drums played at a funeral strongly affect our emotions, although drums usually have only a purely physical effect on the listener. Drawing correct conclusions is sometimes tricky, because generalisations can reveal contradictory elements.

What is in no doubt is that, whatever the type, music has some definite effect, even today, and it is now time we began to make a study of this subject. These stories form a very good basis for such thought, and it now only remains for me, on behalf of all harpers, to give them a very warm welcome, and to add my hope that they will be widely studied, especially by those capable of understanding their hidden meanings. I wish this book much success.

Derek F Bell
Harper to the Chieftains
Bangor, Northern Ireland

Introduction

There has been much debate about the origins of the harp as we know it today, but evidence put forward earlier this year by Keith Sanger and Alison Kinnaird suggests that we owe the form of our modern harp to Scotland rather than Ireland, as had been generally believed, and that it was then disseminated by both cultures across Europe.

Some of these tales are similarly remote in origin, others are relatively recent, and serve to bridge the gap between the harpers of antiquity and the modern day revival of interest in traditional harping. Amongst the older tales, the roots of many of which are untraceable, we find a rich, hidden vein of the universal folk belief in the power of music to affect us on every level of our lives.

These beliefs can be used in various ways. There is a tradition amongst one of the Siberian tribes that a virgin should never bathe alone because of the water spirit; one girl didn't heed the warnings, and did not return until late in the evening, when she claimed that the water spirit had ravaged her while she was bathing. She became pregnant, and later gave birth to a 'spirit' child, which bore a striking resemblance to one of the married men of the village. The possibilities for abuse of the belief will be obvious.

Throughout this collection you will come across a number of references to Fairies. At the risk of being ridiculed, I can honestly say that I believe in the Fairy Folk, by which I mean that other race of beings who live in parallel with ourselves at a higher resonance, and sometimes cross over

into our world. These are not the fanciful sylph-like
fairies who were the inventions of eighteenth century
romanticists.

Half of the stories in this collection are Irish, and still
others have Irish links. The remaining tales are a selection
from various other European and Scandinavian countries.
This choice reflects my own love of these Irish tales, rather
than any paucity of tales from other countries, which in
itself may be a response to the magnificence of the Irish
harping tradition and the importance of the instrument
to the cultural life of the country.

It is a peculiarly Irish paradox that although many of
our finest legends are set in pagan times, they were
meticulously copied down by the monks of the Celtic
church, and it is to them that we are indebted for the
ancient tales that are included here.

During the Middle Ages, especially during the sixth to
eighth centuries, Irish monks spread their faith across
Europe and took a knowledge of their own legendary tales
with them. It is not unlikely that some of the tales that
were later imported into Ireland were variations of the
tales which those early monks had taken with them. Similarly,
it was common for harpers to accompany these monks on
their travels, thus spreading the fame of their harping,
and introducing it into European court life.

One consequence of this cross-fertilisation was that Irish
harpers adopted the European style of playing with the
flesh of their fingers, instead of the nails. Similarly there
was a regular exchange of ideas and tunes between the
harpers of Scotland, Ireland, and to a lesser extent Wales.
There is a tale which explains the origin of the name for
the Welsh harp, telyn; it was originally a derisive nickname
given to the instrument by some Irish harpers who were
brought to Wales by Gruffydd ap Cynan in 1075. The
Welsh harp was strung with horsehair, and the Irish

contemptuously said that it sounded like the buzzing of a bee, which in Irish is teilinn.

The coming of the Normans heralded the end of the professional harper, and Cromwell's policy of harp breaking, along with edicts from the English crown declaring harpers to be outlaws, hastened that decline. By the time of the 1792 gathering of harpers in Belfast the profession was effectively extinct in its earlier form, the status of harper having sunk so low that harping was turned to by those with no other recourse or prospects.

It is ironic then that the lifeline that was thrown to the Irish harpers of the 16th to 18th centuries, should come from the Anglo-Irish nobility. For it was the patronage of a sizeable number of these discerning men and women, around the entire country, that enabled the itinerant harpers to survive. Indeed, if it were not for them, many of the tunes that Edward Bunting collected in Belfast, and over the ensuing years, would have already ceased to exist in Ireland.

The harp is an international instrument, a fact I have attempted to reflect in this collection. Its Irish term is cruit, while in Scotland it is called clarsach, in Wales, telyn or crwth, in Africa, kora, in Korea, kayagum, and in India, vina, and so forth. It is also known in the Old Testament as the kinnor, large harp, or nevel, small harp.

Though harps were rare in Greece and Rome, there is a strong archaeological association between them and the cultures of the Near and Middle East. The harp's literary associations are diverse, ranging from the Northumbrian "Beowulf" to the writings of the 15th century Bengali poet Magh, who describes the six stringed mohati vina, an instrument which held a privileged position in the Hindu culture, and was the focus not only of musical theory but also of semi-philosophical speculations.

In Europe it was essentially a court instrument, so the opportunities for ordinary people to hear it were few and far between. It is not surprising, then, that in Europe it gained the reputation of being an otherworld instrument, and passed into folklore and tradition as an instrument of magic.

The harp is also known in South America but there harp music was the music of the peasantry, and so does not have an association with either nobility or the upper classes, let alone magic. It is not a native instrument, the early South American cultures had no stringed instruments of any kind, so it was perhaps one of the few good things that the Conquistadores brought to those shores.

Among all these lands, with the exception of South America, wherever traces of an earlier naturalistic religion remain, we find the harp commonly represented as a magical instrument, and often as a voice of the Gods. This is perfectly understandable to anyone who has truly felt the power in its music, and whose soul has been touched with awe at that power.

This power has manifested itself in many strange ways. Many people will be unfamiliar with the term 'the music of the spheres', which sounds rather daunting; just as we all have our own individual resonance, a city has a hum, so does the countryside, and so does a planet, while the hum of all the planets together makes the music of the spheres. The idea was first associated in the West with Pythagoras and draws on the ideas of earlier esoteric teachers that sound created form and held the universe together, and that sound is the motivational force behind all energy. According to the beliefs of the African Dogon tribe, music helped to shape the universe and brought order out of chaos.

Of all the arts, music has the most direct effect on human emotions. Music is thus itself an instrument which makes it possible to manipulate individuals and masses. The Orphean bards, were said to legislate through music alone, and the priests of later times took great care to uphold the traditional musical scales, because these, by their resonance, were inclined to invoke corresponding harmonies in the human soul. Innovations in musical form were forbidden because of their disruptive tendencies. As Plato observed, changes in government can be brought about by changes in music.

It has been suggested that where a race has developed to the stage of using a bow and arrow, then stringed instruments are a natural by-product. It was therefore refreshing to read recently of a theory that suggests that the bow was originally a musical instrument. Be that as it may, the interplay between music, passion and violence emerges as an uncomfortably strong theme in these stories.

Another of the main themes running through this collection is the influence of the harp on people's spirituality. There is also a strong sexual undercurrent to many of the tales. Many bards have seen their instrument as a lover, and have immortalised in verse their belief that they would rather have their harp than the love of a woman. An equal number, harpers being restless people, have expressed a desire for both, and have likened their touch upon the strings to a woman's tender caress.

All of the ancient historic instruments have a sexual association: the Grecian god Apollo is commonly depicted with the lyre he invented, but is also known to have had dozens of lovers, both male and female, and interestingly fathered children by both sexes; Bentem the Japanese Shinto goddess of love, beauty, and music, is always shown playing a biwa, which resembles a lute, but she is also known as the White Snake Lady, and the snake is a symbol of fertility and sexuality.

We have one Irish equivalent in the Dagda Mor, who is

associated with the harp. The Dagda had many lovers, including the Boand who is mentioned in "The Sons of Uaithne". He is often represented as having a magic staff, but it is also said of him that his penis was of such proportions that it dragged along the ground and left furrows in the earth. This sounds as if the Dagda was once an agricultural god, who fertilised the earth and, perhaps, used the medium of music to make the seed grow.

While most of the harpers you will meet in this collection are heterosexual, the sexual spectrum represented in these tales is a broad one. Versions of "Prince Edward in the Holy Land", for example, imply that Edward and his harper Robert were sexually intimate. This is not an isolated occurence. The relationship between many harpers and their patrons was ambiguous, to say the least. This is particularly true of the tales from the heroic age, and this should not surprise us, given the polymorphous nature of Celtic sexuality. In many cases this relationship contained a strong homoerotic element and was in some instances openly homosexual. We find an echo of this in the life of O'Carolan, whom I believe to have been homosexual or bisexual, a characteristic he would have had in common with some of his most illustrious predecessors.

Finally, I would like to take this opportunity to thank the staff of the following institutions and organisations for their invaluable assistance: The National Library of Ireland, The Irish Traditional Music Archives, The Royal Society of Antiquaries of Ireland, The British Library, and The Folklore Society Library, London. Thanks also to Jack Hayward, the Celtic Research and Folklore Society, Rabbi Ephraim Mirvis, The Chief Rabbinate of Ireland, Tom Maher, and the members of the Irish Pagan Movement for their support and encouragement.

Russell Walton
Nephin View, County Mayo

The Sons of Uaithne

Ireland

This collection could only begin with this tale. Here we have bound together the birth of three harpers, and the birth of the Irish harping tradition, which required a student to be able to play these three strains of music. The Dagda Mor, the Good God, is the chief deity of the Tuatha de Danann, whose people formed the fifth invasion of Ireland; at least one account has them descending on Slieve Anierin, Co. Leitrim, in the form of a mist. Credited with great magical ability, it is they who are now known as the Fairy Folk, or Sidhe.

It is a distinctive Celtic trait to regard literal truth as being somewhat elastic when it comes to storytelling, and the glorious descriptive passages in this tale are fine examples of this.

I find that I cannot escape the belief that Uaithne was, in fact, another name for the Dagda's harp. Although Uaithne is said to be the Dagda's harper, we have no account of the man himself, which is an unparalleled omission amongst the loquaciousCelts. Of the three different meanings for Uaithne in Old Irish, we may here understand it to be symbolic for harmony in music. The three sacred strains of harping would surely be the natural offspring of that harmony, and the physical manifestation of harmony of spirit, as represented by their Otherworld father, Uaithne.

Uaithne was harper to the Dagda, the Good God of the Tuatha De Danann. It happened that when Uaithne's wife Boand, from whom the River Boyne takes its name, was heavy with child and felt the onset of the first pangs of labour, he played for her upon the Dagda's harp. The harp was crying and moaning with her during the intensity of her pains when her first son was born, so she named him Goltrai, the crying music. It was laughing and joyous with her during the birth of her second son, and so she named him Gentrai, the laughing music. At the birth of her third and last son it was tranquillity itself and so she named him Suantrai, the sleeping music. Then the soothing strains of the harp sent her into a restful sleep after her ordeal. When Boand awoke from her repose, she said to her husband:

"Accept these three fine sons, gentle Uaithne, in return for your generosity. Teach to them all of the fine qualities of harping, that they may follow in your footsteps and be held above all other harpers. But I say now that should they ever go to Magh Cruachan and play at the request of Maeve and Ailill, men will die when they hear their harps."

Now Froech was a chieftain of West Connaught. His mother's name was Bebinn, and she was also of the Tuatha De Danann.

It was Froech's intention to go to Magh Cruachan where Ailill and Maeve, the King and Queen of Connaught, held court, to see for himself the celebrated beauty of their daughter Findabair.

He first went southwards to the Plain of Bregia where the River Boyne flowed, to ask his mother's sister, Boand , for her aid. She equipped Froech and his party handsomely with the weapons and jewels of the Sidhe. She sent three harpers with him too, her own three sons, each with the steeds, arms, dress, appearance and bearing of a king.

This young chief, confident in the splendour of his retinue and in his own beauty of figure, now set out for Magh Cruachan. When they arrived there the party were hospitably received and entertained as honoured guests for some time. During their stay Froech had many opportunities to gaze upon the fair-browed Findabair, who was indeed the fairest maiden that he had ever seen. One evening after a lavish dinner Ailill asked Froech's harpers to play for them.

The three harpers came forward, and this is the way of

When they had finished it was found that twelve men of Ailill's and Maeve's household had died from the intensity of the emotions which the harps had caused within them.

them; they wore grey winding cloaks, with brooches of gold, and their robes were of camlet with silver embroidery upon them. They had circlets of pearls round their heads, rings of gold upon their thumbs, torques of gold around their ears and torques of silver around their throats. Their harps they bore over their shoulders, and this is the way of them; they were carried in harp bags made of the skins of otters studded with coral, with an ornamentation of gold and silver overlay, and lined inside with snow-white roebuck skins; and these again were overlaid with black-grey strips of the softest leather; and a cloth of fine linen, as white as the swan's coat, was wrapped around each string. The harps themselves were made of gold, and silver, and Findruine, with figures of serpents and birds, and greyhounds embossed upon them. These figures were finely made of gold and silver, and as the strings vibrated they ran around the harpers.

Three comely men indeed were these harpers, and pure and sweet was the music which they played. They played long into the night, and their music touched the souls and hearts of all present, and when they had finished it was found that twelve men of Ailill's and Maeve's household had died from the intensity of the emotions which the harps had caused within them.

They were the three sons of Uaithne that were there, and thus the deadly prophecy of Boand came true.

The Great Bardic Company

Ireland

Until the seventh century, Irish poets and bards held substantial privileges. This induced many freeloaders, with little or no talent, to join these professions, so that by 592AD they had reached plague proportions, and were becoming a burden. Seanchan Torpest himself had a reputation for being arrogant and selfish. Although the tale of the first harp is ancient (it echoes belief in nature spirits, bones being a potent magical symbol, with the music being the voice of the wind), it has been drafted into this historical account to help to discredit the intelligence of the bardic class.

When the young Seanchan Torpest had the mantle of chief-poet Ollamh bestowed upon him, he determined to give the honour of his first visit to Gorey, the hospitable King of Connaught. So to Gorey he went with his wife and children, and his accompanying retinue of tutors, pupils, horses, dogs and so forth. They were warmly received and entertained well; but soon some of them began to get very pettish, and to ask for delicacies which were out of season and as such unobtainable.

Their generous host was deeply pained when he found that he could not satisfy the desires of his unreasonable guests. He had a brother named Marbhan, who some years previously had retired from court to the solitude of Glenn Dallun, where he led the life of a recluse, devoting his time to prayer, meditation, and philosophical reflections. To this gifted man the good king went for counsel and assistance in his difficulty; and he was not disappointed, for his brother returned with him shortly afterwards.

Marbhan, having arrived at Gorey's court, introduced himself at once to Seanchan and his learned, though cumbersome, company; and expressed a desire to hear some of their musical performances, both vocal and instrumental, and his wish was freely complied with. The vocalists performed a monotonous toneless chant, which didn't impress Marbhan in the slightest. It wasn't long before he politely suggested he had heard enough.

At this stage one of the company came forward and offered to give him a specimen of his art.

"What is your name, and what art will you display for me?"

"My name is Casmael, and I am first among the harper's of Seanchan's company."

"Will you tell me, Casmael the harper, who made the first harp and what was it made of?"

"I don't know the answer to that."

"Well I know it," said Marbhan, "and I'll tell it to you. There once lived a couple, Cuil the son of Midhuel was the man, and Canoclach Mhor was his wife. They were very happy together in earlier times, but fortune had turned against them so that they were hard pressed now, and each of them began to see faults in the other where none had existed before. As the months passed their bitterness increased, until each of them silently resolved to forsake the other.

Came the early morning of one winter's day and the woman left her hearth and home and fled into the dawn. Soon after, the husband arose and he too set out toward the coming glow. Both of them were ignorant that they each followed the same path. Towards the end of the day the woman came to the sea shore at the mouth of the River Bann, and was walking over the strand when she heard a strange sound which she could not place, a sighing, whispering sound, which seemed to rise and fall on the breeze. She went forward into the wind, seeking the source of the sounds, and came across a skeleton of a whale bleaching in the sun. The wind was shrilling through the sinews of the whale as they hung from the dried bones, and the wild sounds that were produced so enraptured the weary woman that she fell asleep on the strand.

The husband also tracked down the sounds in the wind, and the chords touched him deeply, so that it was some time before he noticed his wife asleep beside the whale. With the uncanny, eldritch notes ringing in his ears, and his soul shaken by an unseen hand, he knew he had wronged his wife, and wished to regain her love. The persistent notes seemed to whisper encouragement to him, and he went into a nearby wood, and crafted a three sided frame from an ancient yew, and he strung it with the sinews of the whale.

When she awoke his wife, too, sought forgiveness and set aside her bitterness. She became his beloved once more, and their days became full of wonder, as the sounds of their harp floated from their home and into the woods, bringing contentment to those whose souls felt its touch.

And that was the first harp that was ever made. But you, the chief harper of this learned company, have no knowledge of it."

Marbhan dealt with the ignorant timpanists and the poets in similar vein, and it soon became apparent to Seanchan's company that they were no match for him, and they put aside their pettishness and superior airs and spent the rest of the visit in agreeable discourse.

Denis Hempson

Ireland

This well known harper lived to the age of 112, a life spanning three centuries, and had the curious habit of taking his harp to bed with him. Among his harp teachers during youth was one of the rare female harpers, Brigid O'Cahan, who may have been related to another great Irish harper, Rory Dall O'Cahan. Hempson lived his later life at Magilligan, by the mouth of the River Bann in Co. Antrim, not far from the setting of our previous tale. Whether or not he, too, came across a stranded whale in his earlier days is not known.

Denis Hempson was born shortly after Turlough O'Carolan, in 1695. In some accounts he is referred to as the man with two heads, due to there being a large excrescence on the back of his head; hence he is always portrayed wearing a hat.

He was in Carolan's company when a youth, but never took pleasure in playing his compositions. The pieces which he delighted to perform were unadorned with modern refinements, which he seemed studiously to avoid, confining himself chiefly to the most antiquated of those airs and melodies which have long survived the memory of their composers, and even a knowledge of the ages that produced them. He was the only one of the harpers at the 1792 meeting in Belfast who plucked the harp with long crooked nails. In playing, he caught the string between the flesh and the nail; not like the other harpers of his day, who pulled it by the fleshy part of the finger alone.

The intricacy and peculiarity of his playing amazed Edward Bunting, who could not avoid seeing it as a vestige of a noble system of practice that had existed for many centuries; strengthening his opinion that the Irish were, at a very early period, superior to the other nations of Europe both in the composition and performance of music.

When visited by Bunting the year after the harp meeting in Belfast, he said to him, with an honest feeling of pride, "When I played the old tunes, not another of the harpers would play after me."

It was with great difficulty that Bunting was able to procure the old harp music from Hempson. When asked to play the very antique tunes, he uniformly replied, "There was no use in doing so, they were too hard to learn, they revived painful recollections." In short he regarded the old music with a superstitious veneration, and thought it in some way a profanation to divulge it to modern ears.

The Harper's Pass

Hebrides

This tale was collected orally on Mull about 1800, and reflects the affection in which the Clarsach is held there to this day. The Hebridean Islands were, and are, one of the strongholds of Gaelic culture. The harper in question may well have been in the employ of the Lords of the Isles, who were the major patrons of all the arts in and around the western Highlands. Such tales as this were popular retellings of actual events, generations old, and served a moral purpose in addition to their historical value.

A number of accounts give the instrument as a timpan. This may be a natural progression, due to the degree of popularity of the different instruments when the separate accounts were noted. As an instrument came more into favour, it tended to adopt the tales told about its predecessor. Most of the tales now told about fiddlers, were originally told about harpers.

The profession of harper was for centuries an exclusively male dominion, and it is not until about four hundred years ago that female harpers are mentioned. Even then they were very much the exception to the rule, Denis Hempson's teacher being one of those exceptions. So most of the harp tales, songs etc. are given from a male viewpoint. Women tend to be portrayed, where they are mentioned at all, as the puppeteer or controller, influencing the train of events but keeping pretty much in the background. Which is surely a departure from the traditions of the Celtic societies, where women, in theory at least, were of equal standing to men.

Near the summit of a steep hill near Moy Castle, in the island of Mull off the west coast of Scotland, there is a gap which has become known as the Harper's Pass.

At one time there was a young woman of exquisite beauty who lived in the isle of Tiree with her mother. She would go anywhere on the isle to listen to songs and stories, and she had a favourite or two with whom to stay the night while she was away. But then her mother died, and she had to go to live on Mull, twenty miles distant, with her grandmother.

There lived in Mull a celebrated harper, and this young woman thought that he would make a fine match for her, on account of his standing. So before the year was out, they were married.

The musician excelled all others in taste and execution; but it was said that he owed a part of his fame to his instrument, for it was so finely made that no artist could hope to equal, much less surpass, it. Next to his wife, it was the pride and joy of his heart, and his companion wherever he went.

One day the couple went to visit a sick relation on the other side of Mull. It was winter, and his wife soon began to sink under the cold. The wind blew keen, making them struggle against the blast, and at last they reached the top of a high hill which they had to cross. Her endurance gave out there, and she fainted from exhaustion. The husband kindled a fire from the dry heath, which was all that grew in that barren soil. But he soon realised that this meagre blaze would not be enough to revive his wife, and that he needed more fuel. Such was his concern and love for her that, without hesitation, he broke his beloved harp into pieces and fed the flames with its fragments.

It was then he saw a stranger out hunting on the hills, and hailed him. His wife recognised the hunter, for he was no stranger to her. For who should he be, but one of her favourites from Tiree. At the sight of this wild, fiery soul, the fine love that had grown between herself and the harper, along with all sense of loyalty, departed her, and she desperately wanted to be with her earlier love.

For his part, he returned her affections and resolved to

carry her off to a distant isle, where they would both be unknown.

The husband was ignorant of all this, and even if he had suspected that they knew each other he would not have acted, for he loved and trusted his wife. But neither his wife nor the hunter gave any indication to him that they knew the other.

When they were rested, the husband thanked the stranger for his assistance, and proposed to his wife that they proceed on their journey. Not wishing to lose sight of the woman, the stranger offered to accompany them for a few miles, just to make sure they were properly recovered, an offer the husband graciously accepted.

Presently, they came to the foot of a mountain, where the woman began to complain of an aching thirst. The husband knew of a stream that ran nearby, and ran to get some water for his beloved wife. When he returned, the shameful pair had eloped.

In the one day the harper had lost both his harp and his wife. In an agony of grief, he cried: "Fool that I was, to burn my harp for you!"

Manannan at Play

Manannan is the sea god of the Tuatha De Danann, MacLir meaning 'Son of the Sea'. Like many of the other De Danann he has come to be portrayed as human, rather than divine. He appears in Irish and Welsh stories and gives his name to Inis Mannan, the Isle of Man.

His bag of crane-skin is said to contain, among other things, the Treasures of the Sea, and we can take this to mean the alphabet secrets of the Peoples of the Sea, namely the Beth-Luis-Nion tree alphabet. The magic herbs he produces from his bag are taken from these trees, but he is not literally administering the herb as a medicine, but is bestowing upon the recipient the wisdom associated with that tree.

Aodh Dubh O'Donnell was holding a feast one time in Bel-atha-Senaig, and his people were boasting amongst themselves of the generosity of their host and the quality of his musicians.

While they were talking, they saw a clown coming towards them. Old striped clothes he had, and puddle water splashing in his shoes, and his sword sticking out naked behind him, and his ears stuck through the old cloak that was over his head, and in his hand he had three spears of holly, all scorched and blackened.

He wished O'Donnell good health, and O'Donnell did the same for him, and asked him where he had come from.

"I slept last night in the palace of the Pictish King of Alba; before that I spent a day in Islay, a day in Kintyre, a day in Rachlainn, and a day in the Watchman's Seat in Slieve Fuaid; I am a rambling, wandering man, and I have come to pay a visit to you, O'Donnell," was the clown's reply.

"Bring the gate-keeper to me," said O'Donnell.

When the man came, he was asked if he had let the clown in, and the gate-keeper replied that he had not, that he had never seen him before.

"Let him off, O'Donnell," said the stranger, "no man saw me come in, and it was as easy for me to come in unseen, as it will be for me to go out again."

There was wonder on the gathering then, that any man could come into the house without passing the gate, and so they knew him to be of the Fairy Folk.

The musicians began playing, and they played very sweet tunes on their harps. But the strange man just called out:

"By my word, O'Donnell, there was never a noise of hammers beating on iron that was as painful to listen to as this din."

With that he drew a harp from under his cloak, and he made music upon it that would put women in a swoon and wounded men after a battle into a sweet sleep, and O'Donnell said of it:

"Since I first heard talk of the music of the Sidhe that is played in the hills and under the earth below us, I never heard better music than your own. It is a very sweet player you are."

"One day I am sweet, another day I am sour," said the clown.

Then O'Donnell bade the clown to sit near him.

"I have no wish to do that," he said, "I would sooner sit here, as an ugly clown, making sport for high-up people."

Then O'Donnell sent him down some new clothes, a hat and a striped shirt and a coat, but he would not have them.

"I have no intention," he said, "of letting high-up people be making a boast of giving them to me."

They were afraid then that he might leave them without offering gifts in return, and they put twenty armed horsemen and twenty men on foot to keep him from leaving the house, and as many more outside the gate.

"What are these men for?" said he.

"They are to keep you here, until we find out just who, and what, you are," said O'Donnell.

"By my word, you are ill-mannered, it is not with you I will be eating my supper tomorrow," he said, "but at Knockainey Hill with Seaghan, son of the Earl of Desmond."

"If you try and move from this place between now and tomorrow morning, I will knock you into a round lump and play hurley with your head," said O'Donnell.

At that the stranger took up the harp again, and he made the same sweet music as before. And when they were all listening to him, he called out to the men outside:

"Here I come, and watch me well now or you will lose me."

When the men that were watching the gate heard that, they lifted up their axes to strike him down, but in their haste it was at one another they struck, till they were all lying stretched in blood. Then the clown said to the gate-keeper:

"Go and ask O'Donnell for twenty cows and a hundred of free land, as a fee for bringing his people back to life. If you take this herb, and rub it in the mouth of each man, he will rise up whole and well again."

So the gate-keeper did that, and he received the cows and the land from O'Donnell gladly, and he brought all the men back to life again. But they could not find the clown.

Now at the time that O'Donnell's men were searching for the clown, Seaghan was holding a gathering on the green in front of his dun, and he saw the same man coming towards him, and dressed in the same way, and

the water splashing in his shoes. But when he asked who
the newcomer might be, he gave himself the name of a
very learned man, Duartane O'Duartane, and he said it
was by the falls of Eas Aodha Ruaidh on the River Erne he
had come, and by Ceischorainn and from that to Corrslieve,
on to the plain of Magh Lorg of the Dagda, thence into
the district of Hy'Conaill Gabhra, until he had come to
Seaghan's own dun by Cruachan of Magh Aoi.

So they brought him into the house and gave him wine
for drinking and water for washing his feet, and he slept
till the rising of the sun on the morrow. Soon after dawn
Seaghan came to visit him, and said:

"It is a long sleep you have had, and there is no wonder
in that, with your journey so long yesterday. I have often
heard of your great learning in books and of your skill on
the harp, and I would very much like to listen to you this
morning."

"I am good in those arts indeed," said the stranger.

So they brought him a book, but he could not read a
word of it, and then they brought him a harp, and he
could not play any tune.

"It seems your reading and your music have deserted
you," said Seaghan.

So he composed a short verse about him, saying it was a
strange thing for Duartane O'Duartane, who had such a
great name, not to be able to read a line of a book, or even
to remember one, and not to be able to put two notes
together on the harp. But when the stranger heard how
he was being mocked, he took up the book, and read from
the top to the bottom of the page very well and in a clear,
sweet-sounding voice. After that he took up the harp and
played and sang the same wondrous tunes as he had at
O'Donnell's house the day before.

"It is a very sweet man of learning you are," said Seaghan.

"One day I am sweet, another day I am sour," said the stranger.

They walked out together then on Knockainey, but while they were talking there, the stranger suddenly vanished, and Seaghan did not know where he had gone.

That is the way in which Manannan MacLir used to go round Ireland, doing tricks and wonders. Nobody could keep him in any place, and if he was put on the gallows themselves, he would be found safe in the house afterwards, and some other man on the gallows in his place. But he did no real harm, and those he put to death, he would bring to life again with a magic herb from his crane-skin bag.

The Lover's Harp

Iceland

Originally this tale was told in the form of an Icelandic poem, and its theme is echoed in a traditional English folk song, "The Two Sisters", as well as another from Scotland, "The Twa Sisters".

At one time it was believed that the soul resided in the bones and hair. So making an instrument from these was akin to giving the living soul a new voice. Sometimes the finger bones of the corpse were used as tuning pins, or as a tuning key.

Given that the northern counties of England, and parts of Scotland and the Isles, were for hundreds of years under Viking influence or control, the Icelandic version was probably brought to those shores with the invaders, and adapted to local use.

In Vadil in the Westfjords in Iceland there once lived two beautiful sisters, Signy and Hilda. Signy was the younger and her heart was as pure as the gold of her flaxen hair, while Hilda's hair was raven dark, and her heart was as black as mould.

A chieftain's son came from the Althing at Thingvellir to seek a wife, and faced with the choice between the two, he courted the younger one. After some weeks of this, Hilda said to her kindly sister: "Dear Signy, let's go for a walk beside Thorskfjord".

They wandered down to the shore, Signy unsuspecting of the darkness in her sister's soul. When they came to a place where the tide ran swift, Hilda hurled her sister in. Signy reached up her delicate white hand and cried: "Sister, please help me back to land."

But wicked Hilda just sneered and said: "It isn't I who'll

When they came to a place where the tide ran swift,
Hilda hurled her sister in.

help you back to land, unless you give your gold shoes to me."

"My golden shoes I'll gladly give, if you help me reach the land again."

"Before I risk my own dear neck for one such as you, you must give me your wealth and beauty too."

"My wealth you may have, but my beauty isn't mine to give, but it is yours if the Gods so wish it."

"Before I help you to the shore, you must give me your lover's firm, strong hand."

"All I can give I'll gladly give to you, but I cannot give something that belongs to my lover."

With this Hilda stood back and watched the currents take her sister out from the shelter of the fjord, and into the open sea, where the waves swept her body into the ocean depths. Hilda returned home and told all of the tragic death of Signy, saying that she had thrown herself from the cliffs in despair. The chieftain's son now turned his attentions to Hilda, and ere long a wedding feast was being prepared.

But the sea grew restless holding the body of poor wronged Signy. The winds blew and the clouds billowed black, and her battered body was swept landwards.

Before he took his marriage vows, the lover walked down along the sand where, to his great pain, he found Signy's body washed up onto the shore. Laying her white body in the shade of some trees, he cut three strands of her golden hair, and spun three harp strings long and fair. Of her breastbones he fashioned a harp, and with this he returned to the feasting.

He struck the first string, and it cried: "I once had a sister, but she is now this bride."

He struck the next string and it told the first: "She is the one who robbed me of my lover."

When he struck the third string it answered them both:

"This bride is the one who caused my death."

The chieftain's son now struck the harp with all his might, and the wicked bride's heart broke with grief at her misfortune. Not a remorseful thought did she have even then.

They recovered Signy's body, and it was buried in warm, packed earth, with twelve fine noblemen standing round to pay their respects. Hilda was buried among cold, hard rocks, with no one deeming it worthy to honour her, and people say her troubled spirit walks there still.

The lover forsook his claim to the chieftainship, and fulfilled his passion for his murdered love by spending the rest of his days travelling between the far flung farms of Iceland, carrying the harp made of the bones of Signy, and all who heard it marvelled at the purity of its voice.

The Blind Romeo

The bonds of friendship that existed among the itinerant harpers were rarely as strong as on this occasion, and it is a pity that we know little else about these two harpers than is given here. Keenan was obviously an athletic individual, and I think it was this rather than his music which inclined the governess towards him.

Owen Keenan was a blind harper who regularly played at the residence of the Stewart family near Cookstown, Co. Tyrone. There was a French governess residing with them, and Keenan was so carried away by his feelings for her that, one night, he stole a ladder and climbed in through her bedroom window. The governess had always viewed Keenan with a simmering passion, so it was hardly surprising that they were found exhausted in each others arms the following morning. This so deeply offended Mr Stewart that he had Keenan committed to Omagh gaol on the charge of housebreaking, which was the only illegal thing he had done.

At that time, in the Barony of Tirawley, Co. Mayo, there lived a very good blind harper called Hugh Higgins. He was the embodiment of a gentleman harper, was uncommonly genteel in his manners, and spared no expense in his dress. He travelled in such a manner as did, and always will do, credit to an Irish harper. On hearing of Keenan's misfortune he set out for Omagh with some of his followers. When he arrived at the gaol he found that the keeper was away, and that his wife was left in charge of the prisoner, but Higgins' fine appearance and retinue readily gained him admission to the gaol. Now the gaoler's wife was a virtuous woman, but she had three great weaknesses, music, wine, and above all flattery, for although she was now well past her prime she had once been thought a great beauty.

Higgins hadn't been there an hour before his charm asserted itself over the poor woman, and she readily accepted his offer of wine for herself and the turnkeys, who couldn't believe their luck, and were soon so drunk that they would not have noticed if the gaol had burnt down around them.

Higgins began to play for her, and she soon fell under the spell of the music and the wine. So she didn't notice when Higgins slipped the keys to Keenan, who released himself and marched out into the moonlight, with a boy of Higgins' on his back to guide him over a ford of the River Strule, which flowed beside the gaol.

After playing on for some time Higgins left the besotted woman asleep in her chair, and made haste for home before the deed was discovered. Owen Keenan, meanwhile, went direct to Cookstown to see his lover. He scaled the walls to her bedroom once more and, before the dawn could betray them, carried her off, and he married her soon after.

They both emigrated on the next available ship to the United States, where it is said that Keenan's French wife took advantage of his blindness and repeatedly proved unfaithful.

The Song of Gunnar

Denmark

This tale forms an offshoot of the Volsunga Saga, and can equally be attributed to Germany as Denmark, the Saga being common to both countries.

Gunnar was the last of the race that plundered the Niebelung horde from the depths of the Rhine. In some accounts he is still bound when he is pushed into the pit and plays the harp with his feet.

The power of music is here used to illustrate the ascendancy of the northern Odinist Gods over an older pantheon. All of the snakes are charmed into slumber by the music, bar one, a serpent left over from the birth of the human world, Midgard. Unable to overcome the Odin-inspired music, he bides his time until the coming dawn, a time when night and day are in transition, when Gunnar's magic is weakest.

Gudrun was a Princess of the Rhinelands, the wife of Sigurd the dragon-slayer, and her pride in his fame made her arrogant and haughty. One day, while she was bathing in the river with Brynhild, the wife of her brother Gunnar, she taunted Brynhild about how much braver her husband was than Gunnar, who was himself a champion. Brynhild told Gunnar what had been said, declaring that while Sigurd was alive she would be unable to consider him worthy of her love, and would no longer be his wife. Incensed, Gunnar arranged for his two brothers to slay Sigurd while he slept, which they did by plunging a sword between his shoulder blades.

Gudrun too was in fear of Gunnar's wrath, and fled southward until she reached Verona, where she was captured by Attila, chief of the Huns. She sought the protection of this great warrior and became one of his many wives, serving him faithfully.

On hearing of this, Gunnar and his brothers gathered a select band of men, and set out to reclaim their sister from the Hun, claiming the right of vengeance against her themselves. One brother was slain early in their march, and when Gunnar and his remaining brother came upon the army of Attila, their men were killed and they were taken captive.

Both men were marched in chains to Attila's stronghold in Wallachia, where they were brought into his presence. Not a word did Gudrun speak in their favour, for she knew what her fate at their hands would be, and when Gunnar's brother was brought forward, and because he was bound and no threat to her, she slew him herself. Only Gunnar now remained, and he was brought forward and spoke to Attila:

"Lord of the Eastlands," he began, "I am the only one left now to tell of the ransom of Odin that once lay deep in the waters, but let it lie in the waters again, let the Gods be rich and in peace! I am the last of my line, and the words and the babble of life that surround me will soon cease, and I welcome the silence."

Attila respected these as the words of a brave man, for here was a warrior who did not shrink from death. And his was to be a death that time would remember.

Gunnar was seized and carried out into the camp, where the moonlight glittered off the weapons of the surrounding host. When he was placed upon a hay wagon Gunnar looked to the heavens and called to his Gods, and welcomed the immediate relief of rain. Burning was not to be his fate. A wise man amongst the swordsmen loosened his bonds, and commanded his harp to be brought and laid by his side. Then he was taken to a deep circular pit, which was home to the deadliest of serpents. Gunnar's hands were freed and his harp placed between them, then he was flung into the pit. The bottom of the pit still retained the heat of the day, and Gunnar sat on a rock in the middle. The serpents crept nearer, so he rose to his feet and struck the harp, and it rang with the cry of the lost.

He fondled its strings through the night, and the coils of death were stayed. Then up rose the Song of Gunnar, a great mystical song that told of the world at its birth. Great grew the voice of Gunnar, and his speech hung sweet on the winds.

Then his voice grew low, and he sang of the deeds of his life: "Hearken kings and nations of this bountiful earth, pay heed to my words those still unborn. I have lived in this world before, and I called it a Garden of the Gods; I have refreshed my heart with its sweetness, and trodden its freshness underfoot; I have beheld its fury and been awed, and welcomed the new dawning sun; I have dealt with the deeds of the mighty; I have woven the web of the sword; and I fought and was glad in the morning, and sing in the night at the end."

The speech of Gunnar fell away, but his nimble hands were still busy upon the harp. The crests of the serpents had fallen, and their flickering tongues were still. The Roller and the Coiler, and Greyback, the lord of ill, Grave-groper and Death-swaddler, the Slumberer of the Heath, Gold-wallower, Venom-smiter, and the loose coils of Long-back, all lay silent and still, as fattened cows in the summer heat. All save the Grey and Ancient, that creature from Midgard's birth, who held his crest aloft.

The dark of night was waning, and the chill of dawn was creeping over the land, when the harp grew faint and slow, and the Serpent lashed at Gunnar. His hands awoke the fainting harp, and once more his song broke forth:

"I see the spring of the day round the doors of golden Valhalla, and I hear the voice of Odin, and the call of the

Valkyrie for me. Odin, I see and I hear, but I must be free of this body, before we meet in your land. I crave peace and am weary, Allfather, and long and dark is the road, the feet of the mighty are weakened, and my back is bent with the load." Then the Song of Gunnar faded, and the harp fell from his hands: "Cold is the heart within me, and my hand is heavy and dark, come for me God of the war-fain for my death is surely at hand." He fell to the earth as he spoke, and the life left brave Gunnar, for his heart and harp were stilled forever by the sleepless worm's venom.

The moon was low in the heavens, and the sun was rising in the East, and the light clouds cast speeding wraiths over the body of the fallen hero.

Reverend Charles Bunworth

Ireland

The good Reverend was somewhat more fortunate than Gunnar, in that he was able to live out his allotted span in peace; at least with as much peace as a clergyman is likely to get.

He was one of a number of landowners who actively supported and encouraged the travelling harpers. It is largely due to the efforts of these men and women from the Anglo-Irish gentry and those of Presbyterian antiquarians that the spirit of the Gaelic harping tradition was kept alive, when it could have been lost forever.

The Rev. Charles Bunworth was rector of Buttevant, Co. Cork, about the middle of the eighteenth century. He was the ideal of what a man of the cloth should be like, but what so many are not. A learned man of unaffected piety; pure in heart and benevolent in intention, he was respected by the gentry and beloved by the poor folk, regardless of their faith, for they knew that in matters of difficulty and in seasons of distress they could be confident of receiving from him the advice and assistance that a father would afford to his children.

But what extended the fame of Mr Bunworth far beyond the limits of his neighbouring parishes, was his innate ability on the Irish harp, and his hospitable reception and entertainment of the poor itinerant harpers who travelled from house to house about the country. His kindness and generosity did not go unrewarded, as the minstrels sang his praises to the tingling accompaniment of their harps, invoking abundant blessings upon his head in return for his bounty, and celebrating in their verses the blooming charms of his young daughters, Elizabeth and Mary. It was all these poor harpers could do; but who can doubt that their gratitude was sincere, for at the time of Mr Bunworth's death, no less than fifteen harps had been deposited on the loft of his granary, bequeathed to him by the last members of a race which has now ceased to exist.

The value of these harps is irrelevant, for there is something in a gift of the heart which merits preservation. However, soon after the death of Mr Bunworth, his family moved to Cork for a temporary change of scene, and left the house in the hands of an ignorant family follower, and one by one the harps were broken up to feed his cooking fires.

The Harp of the Dagda Mor

Ireland

This is probably the best known of the Irish legends concerning harps, and is closely related to "The Sons of Uaithne". Our first tale showed how the three strains of music came to be named, and if we accept that Uaithne was the third name of the Dagda's harp, then he is here depicted as channelling his powers of music into our world through his children, the three sacred strains.

All of the Tuatha De Danann are Gods but, like many Gods before them, they have become rationalised into mortal men by scribes who did not understand their purpose. Although the Dagda is often portrayed as the leader of the De Danann, he is also a Master of the druidic arts and husband to the Morrigan, goddess of battle, whilst Ogma is the De Danann champion, and Lugh is their leader in preparations for battle, as well as being Master of all the arts and sciences.

The Dagda is also father to Brigit, goddess of poetry, smithcraft and healing, who later became Christianised into St Brigid. The St Brigid's crosses that are to be found in so many homes can equally be associated with Brigit, the threefold pagan Goddess.

Following their victory over the Fomoire at the second battle of Moytura, the Tuatha De Danann came together to celebrate their triumph.

As the champions and heroes gathered in the banquet hall for their great feasting, there was a call for music from the harp of that great warrior, the Dagda Mor. The Dagda went to fetch it, but found that his beloved harp had been stolen.

"An evil thing has come to pass," said the Dagda when he returned. "The vile Fomorach have laid hands upon my sweet-tongued harp and borne it away; but it shall be a silent mouth to them, until I find it. Who will join me in bringing back that heavenly tree?"

Then the champions Ogma and Lugh arose from their feasting and said: "We will join you in your quest, even if we have to travel over hills of glass and across lakes of smothering fire."

They sharpened their spears until sparks of fire ran along their edges, and polished their shields so that they captured the light of the dying sun, then charged once more with the fire of battle, they set out after the Fomorach. They went without ceasing from nightfall to nightfall; they crossed nine high hills, where only the mountain heathers grew, and nine dark valleys, where the blaze of their shields pushed back the shadows, and they forded nine broad river mouths, where none but the brave could cross.

They found the remains of the Fomorach host camped in a remote glen. But though they were eating and drinking the Fomorach had not the consolation of either music or storytelling, and the heaviness of defeat lay upon them all like a shroud.

In the midst of them lay the harp of the Dagda; a silent mouth, for not even the most skilful of the Fomorach minstrels could draw music from it, on account of the Dagda having bound its melodies.

Such was the gloom within the Fomorach camp that they did not see the approaching warriors until they stood in their very midst, where the brilliance of their presence could not be ignored. But the Dagda scorned to acknowledge his enemies, and when he saw his harp laying neglected on the cold ground his eyes became like sparks of lightning, he opened wide his arms and called:

> Come Daur Da Blao,
> Come Coir Cetharchair,
>
> Come Summer, Come Winter,
> Mouths of harps and bags and pipes!

The harp sprang from its place. Nine of the Fomorach rose up to stop its escape; and its touch was death for each of them. It leapt to the bosom of the Dagda Mor, like a son running to its father, or a maid to her sweetheart. He cradled it in his arm and drew his hand over the strings and played the 'Goltrai', the sorrowful music. It was then that the Fomorach, both men and women, forgot their hatred and their battle fury. The warriors drew their mantles over their faces to hide the shame of their weeping, while the women wept three showers of tears, so heart-rending were the strains of the magic harp.

"Play them a different kind of music," said Ogma, "they have no spirit left, and I think that they have suffered enough."

"I will do that," answered the Dagda Mor.

Then he drew his hand over the strings again, and he played the 'Gentrai', the joyful music, until the men and the women shouted and laughed with delight at the sheer joy of it. Such was its power that if every man and woman in Eire had had their father and mother lying dead before them, they would have had to laugh with gladness for that melody.

"Play the 'Suantrai' for them," said Lugh, "then we can return to our companions."

"I can do that, and none better than myself to do it," answered the Dagda.

Then he swept his hands over the strings of the harp once more, and it answered him with the music of sleep. Creeping, crooning, soothing strains of murmurous music it played for him, until the heads of all the Fomorach warriors fell upon their breasts, and their women sank to the floor in deep and heavy slumber.

The Dagda Mor carried his harp forth into the darkness, and returned with Ogma and Lugh to his own people. That was the last time there was a battle between the

Fomorach and the Tuatha De Danann, the Fairy Folk of the Goddess Danu.

The kingship and sovereignty of the island remained with them, until the sons of Milidh came over the seas, and drove them into the raths and Sidhe-mounds where they live to this day, an invisible, enchanted people.

Turlough O'Carolan

Certain authors have recently attempted to turn this celebrated harper-composer into a mystic figure, endowing him with the power of voice control over his harp, even suggesting that it would play only for him, as in the case of the Dagda Mor. Unfortunately for history, the only similarity between the characters of O'Carolan and the Dagda Mor, is their self-professed fondness for strong drink.

O'Carolan was born into a poor family in the year 1670, in the townland of Spiddal, along the main road from Kells to Nobber.

When still a young man and in full possession of his eyesight he fell in love with Brigid Cruice, and she returned his affection. Her family, however, owned a large amount of property in that area, and as they wished her to find a wealthy husband, they scorned the match between Brigid and O'Carolan, and they banished him from their lands.

Not long after this O'Carolan was stricken by smallpox and became blind, causing him to take up the harp, and eventually to make his way as an itinerant harper. He was never more than merely proficient on the harp; it was his compositions which marked him out from his contemporaries, but even these did not meet with universal acclaim at the time. He was also known to have an uncertain temper.

One night when O'Carolan was sitting in a bar in Castleblayney, Co. Monaghan, another blind harper by the name of John Murphy strutted in, and made some derogatory comments about his compositions, saying that they were like "bones without meat".

"Damn me," says O'Carolan, "but I'll compose a tune before I quit you, and you may put what meat you please on the bones of it." With that he left his seat, and cautiously stealing behind Murphy seized him by the hair of his head, and dragged and kicked him about the room unmercifully. Murphy's screeches could be heard at a great distance; and all the time O'Carolan was shouting at him, "Put beef to that air, you puppy." If the landlord hadn't decided that Murphy had had enough there wouldn't have been a drop of blood left in the impudent fellow. It was about this time that O'Carolan composed his "Receipt for Drinking Whiskey".

O'Carolan also had an amazing ability to commit tunes to memory, as well as being able to produce new melodies with astonishing ease. Once he was at the house of an Irish nobleman where the famous Italian composer Geminiani was present, and O'Carolan challenged him to a trial of skill. Geminiani responded by playing the fifth concerto of Vivaldi on his violin, which O'Carolan instantly repeated on his harp, despite his never having heard it before then. The surprise of the gathering was increased when he boldly stated that he could compose a concerto himself that very night, which he did by using the buttons of his coat, taking them as representative of the lines and spaces in musical notation; and the piece has ever since been known as "O'Carolan's Concerto".

Cornelius Lyons, household harper to the Earl of Antrim, was a friend and rival to O'Carolan in his art and composition. He was also able to see perfectly, unlike many other harpers. It happened once that Lyons was at the home of a Mr Archdall, in Co. Fermanagh, when O'Carolan was also there. Lyons overheard him composing the tune "Mrs Archdall", and as O'Carolan could not see him, Lyons wrote down the music as fast as O'Carolan composed it. Mr Archdall and Lyons then planned a joke

Stealing behind Murphy, he seized him by the hair of his head...

at O'Carolan's expense.

There was another itinerant harper by the name of Charles Berreen, and O'Carolan detested him, because he was but a poor harper and without any ability in composition. Knowing this to be the case, Mr Archdall, the following day, threw up the window of the sitting room and exclaimed: "Upon my word, here is Berreen coming", which vexed O'Carolan very much. But upon the protests of Mr Archdall concerning hospitality, and the crime attached to the breach of it, O'Carolan consented to his supposed admission.

Lyons had a servant named McDermott, who could play quite well on the harp and had a fine sense of humour. Lyons and McDermott went into the hall where Lyons took the harp, and McDermott placed himself behind his master to answer any questions which O'Carolan might put to the supposed Berreen, O'Carolan knowing his friend Lyons' voice too well.

Lyons began to play the tune of "Mrs Archdall" in the poorest manner he could, to imitate Berreen, and McDermott counterfeited his voice. At this the hot tempered O'Carolan began to prance and dance with madness about the parlour and roared out to the supposed Berreen to know where he had got the tune.

"Oh," says McDermott, "I have had that tune ten years or more."

"You are a damned liar and a scoundrel," exclaimed O'Carolan, "and even if it was the devil that taught you, you have it only since last night."

There was a public stocks near the house and O'Carolan told Mr Archdall that if Berreen was not immediately put into them he would never come near his house again, on which McDermott pretended to make a loud and strong resistance, but was taken to the stocks where he sat down and a noise was made as of putting in his legs.

But O'Carolan was not yet satisfied without beating the plagiarist, and made a great blow of his cane at him, which McDermott fortunately avoided. At last O'Carolan suspected that he had been tricked, and seemed so unhappy that Mr Archdall and Lyons explained the whole thing to him. When he had heard all, he laughed and shook hands with Mr Archdall, thanking him for his usual good humour.

In his later years he went on a pilgrimage to Lough Derg; and a woman offered her hand to help him into the boat, and when he caught hold of her hand he said that he was holding the hand of Brigid Cruice, and he was. He had never forgotten his love of forty years earlier.

This remarkable musician died on Saturday March 25th 1738, at the age of sixty-eight, and his last act was to perform a wild and touching "Farewell to Music", upon his beloved harp.

Heinrich Frauenlob

Germany

I find myself torn between two conceptions of this interesting man: on the one hand there is the genuine lover of women, and on the other we have a cassocked Casanova whose love was far from pure or true. We know that music can be a powerful tool for seduction, and it appears that Heinrich was also aware of that. His very name points towards this interpretation; Frauenlob meaning 'Lover of Women'.

Heinrich of Meissen was a priest in the town of Mayence. He was a fine, worthy man, and possessed of a gifted voice, and he loved to play the harp, and wrote many fine songs in honour of beautiful women, and the female sex in general.

The title of woman, Heinrich considered higher than that of wife, which only signifies a married woman. On account of the chivalry displayed in his many poems and songs, history has given him the name by which he was best known, "Frauenlob".

Frauenlob was loved and venerated by many women in life, and also in death. His funeral cortege was composed mainly of women in deep mourning, and eight of the most beautiful among them carried the coffin, upon which was placed his harp covered with sweet scented flowers. Rhine wine, which had so often inspired his poetry, was poured into his grave, and the countless precious tears which covered his coffin were shed by many a gentle lady.

The Living Harp

Finland

This tale is found in various forms throughout Europe. Usually the hero has to first build a fabulous bridge overnight, then to find some buried pigs, before being given a third seemingly impossible task. Originally the bridge may have been representative of a rainbow, linking earth and sky, thus providing a bridge into the next world, while pigs are associated with the Underworld so can be taken as symbols of death. Bringing the Living Harp into the human world, and through it the wonder of music, is a worthy task for anyone, and by completing this task the young man would have secured his passage over the rainbow, and avoided the tortures that waited below.

Harps are commonly made of willow, so it is interesting to note that this harp is made of pine. Perhaps, among the northern Scandinavians, pine was a more magical wood than the willow, which in warmer climes is held sacred to the Goddess.

There was once an old widow woman whose only joy was her fine son, who cared for her. But for two days nothing had fallen to the young man's gun, and they were hungry. So it was that on the third morning he set out with little enthusiasm for the hunt. He wandered about for many hours without seeing a thing, but just as dusk was falling, he saw a squirrel in a tree. He lifted his gun to shoot it, but the little creature cried: "Don't shoot me! Don't shoot me!" in such a pleading tone that his heart was touched with pity.

"All right, I won't kill you," he said, and the squirrel ran down the tree towards him. But no sooner had it touched the ground than it changed into the loveliest girl he had ever seen. Her eyes were like stars and her hair floated round her like a golden mist, and her voice was more delicate than the sweetest of birds.

"Thank you for sparing my life," she said. "Now it is yours, and you may claim me as your bride."

He took her by the hand and led her to his house. The widow did not know what to think of it at first, but when she came to know the beautiful girl she could not refuse. So they were married and lived very happily for some time.

Now it so happened that the King's son was seeking a bride, and though he had met many lovely maidens from the very finest families, he could not find one to suit him. One day he was riding through the forest, and he chanced to come past the widow's house where he saw the beautiful young bride and fell in love with her at once. He determined to have her for his own, and made up his mind to destroy the husband, so he sent for the young man, and said to him: "I have a task for you, which you must perform, or I will cut off your head. You must go to the rapids and build a golden bridge over them, with silver railings to support it, and if it is not done by the day after tomorrow you will die."

The poor young man was very frightened, for he had no means of doing such a thing, and when he went home he was very sad. His wife asked him what was the matter, and when he had told her, she said: "Let us lie down and sleep. We shall know more in the morning."

The next day, when they woke, she gave him a silk handkerchief.

"Take this," she said, "strike the rapids with it, and command a golden bridge with silver railings to rise in the night."

He did as she told him, and next morning, when the King's son went to look, there was a fine bridge of gold flashing in the sunlight.

The young man thought he would be left in peace now, but it was not to be, for the false prince was determined to destroy him. He sent for him again and said: "I have another task for you. There are three golden pigs buried somewhere in this garden, and you must find them before the day after tomorrow, or I will cut off your head."

The lad went back to his wife and asked her advice, and they laid down together to sleep as before. In the morning she said: "You must go to the King's son and ask that one of his generals shall accompany you on your search. Then you must take a spade and dig under the oak tree that stands in the middle of the garden, and there you will find the pigs in a deep pit."

Her husband went back to the prince and asked that one of his generals should go with him, and the two men went together to the garden. They dug under the oak, and there they found the pigs, exactly as the bride had foretold. The prince was not at all pleased, and now he thought of a third task, even harder than the others. He said he wished to have a harp that would play of itself, without the hand of any musician upon it. The young man said that such a thing did not exist, but the King's son said he must find one, or he would lose his head.

When the bride heard of this, they lay down to sleep together, and in the morning she told him to return to the King's son and ask for three months and a day to find the Living Harp. Moreover, he was to take with him three of the most important generals, and they must all come back to her before they set out. The prince was obliged to agree to these conditions, and on the following day the four men prepared to start on their journey. As soon as the sun rose the bride gave them some food in a knapsack, and then she took her husband aside and gave him a silk handkerchief.

"You will come to one place," she said, "and there you

must show it, and you will come to another, and you must show it again. But do not show it a third time unless you are in peril of your life."

Then she kissed him tenderly and threw a ball of blue thread out of the door, telling him to follow it wherever it went, and he would find the harp.

The ball rolled along the ground, and the four men followed it all through the day. The sun set and the stars came out, and the ball stopped at the door of a little earth covered hut, so they went in. An old, old woman was sitting inside, and when she saw them, she said: "I have not smelt human flesh for thirty long years, but now I shall have a good supper at last."

The generals were greatly alarmed at this saying, but the young man took out the silk handkerchief and wiped his face. The old crone looked at him and said: "Now I see who you are, for it is my daughter's husband who stands before me."

She got up from her seat and brought them food and drink, and afterwards she gave them soft beds to lie on, and everything they could wish for. They stayed there for the night, and the next day they went on again, following the blue ball as before. In the evening it led them to another earth covered hut where an old woman was sitting, even more ancient than the last. She looked very pleased at the sight of them, and said:

"I have not smelt human flesh for sixty long years, but now I shall have a good supper at last."

However, she did not eat them, for when she saw the silk handkerchief she said the lad was the husband of her niece. She entertained them right royally, and they slept there that night very comfortably.

When the sun rose the blue ball ran before them, and they followed it over hill and dale until they came to another hut in the evening. They saw a woman so old that

the mountains were young beside her, and she prepared
to eat them at once, for she said she had not smelt human
flesh for ninety long years.

"Nay now, mother," said the young man. "Surely you
will not eat four poor travellers? We have journeyed so far
and so fast that our flesh is as tough as leather, and the
soup from our bones would be nothing but dishwater."

She hesitated at that, and presently she said that they
might stay there if they liked, but she could give them
nothing to eat. So they sat down and ate the food that the
bride had given them, and the young man told the old
woman they were looking for a harp that would play of
itself.

"My sons could make it for you," she said, "but they will
not be at home before darkness falls again."

The travellers said they would wait for them, and sure
enough, when darkness fell again, three savage wolves
came bounding through the roof. They leapt to the ground
and changed into young men in fine garments. They
agreed to make the harp, but said that someone must
hold the pineboard for them. One of the generals took it,
and the wolf-sons said he must keep awake whatever he
did, or it would be the worse for him. The general said
that was easy, but he soon found it was not, for he began
to feel drowsy. Before long he was sound asleep, and the
three wolves ate him up and ran out of the hut. The next
night another general held the board, but he too slept
and was eaten, and the same thing happened to the third.
So now there was no one left but the young man.

When night fell the wolves returned and told him to
take up the pineboard and not to sleep whatever he did,
or it would be the worse for him. They worked away at the
harp, and the poor lad felt sleepier and sleepier. Every
now and then one of the wolf-sons said, "Are you asleep?",
and he answered, "No," but he felt it would not be long

before he was. At last he could bear it no longer, so he said: "I want to know whether there is more dry wood than green in the forest."

"We will find out," said the wolves, and they bounded away to count the trees. They counted and counted all day long, and it was not until dusk that they leapt through the roof again. Then they told him to take up the board, and they worked away at the harp, while he grew sleepier and sleepier every moment. "Are you awake?" they kept saying, and though he answered "Yes" every time, he knew that he would soon fall asleep and be eaten. He felt that he was in peril of his life, so he drew out the silk handkerchief and wiped his face with it. At once the old woman said:

"The husband of my niece stands before me. Why did you not tell me who you were before? The harp would have been finished long ago had I known."

She bustled about and gave him rich foods to eat, and the three wolf-sons finished the harp in a trice. It sang by itself as sweetly as a running stream, and its lovely music filled the hut and the forest till the birds stopped singing from sheer envy.

As soon as it was ready the old woman told her sons to take up the young man on their backs and carry him home.

"Away with you," she said, "for even now the King's son has stolen my niece, and is forcing her to marry him."

The lad mounted the wolves, and away they went through the dark trees as swiftly as the wind. They went straight to the house of the King's son, and there they found everyone running to and fro in great haste. The cooks were baking, the maidens were spinning, the servants were putting up fine hangings of red and blue in the hall. The prince had stolen the beautiful bride and was forcing her to marry him in the morning, so the wedding feast was being prepared. The young man rushed into the room and flung down the

*The lad mounted the wolves, and away they went through
the dark trees, as swiftly as the wind.*

harp before the prince.

"False deceiver," he cried, "you have broken your word. You promised me three months and a day to find the harp, but you have stolen my wife before the time was ended."

The King's son was very ashamed before all his followers, and he had to let the girl go. So the young man took his lovely wife home again to his mother's house, and there they lived happily together for the rest of their lives, without anyone to trouble them.

Christina Hole

Maon & Craiftine

Ireland

The first part of this tale is thought to date back to about 500BC, and centres on the events leading up to the destruction of Dindrigh. It was only natural that Maon should go to France, because there was then a friendly alliance between the Leinstermen and the French, just as between the Connaughtmen and the Welsh, indeed, every province in Ireland had a similar overseas alliance. Some versions introduce the three strains of harping as being used to overcome the defenders' resistance. I think this has been added later.

That the first 'suitable tree' that Craiftne comes on is a willow is no coincidence. Harps were often made of willow because it possessed the right tonal qualities. The willow was also revered as the tree of enchantment, and was held as being sacred to the moon. Interestingly enough, when the Israelites were held captive in Babylon and were jeeringly asked to sing the songs of Zion, they responded by refusing and hanging their harps on willow trees.

The second part of the tale is also a later addition, a ruler with a horse's or ass's ears being a common theme in many lands, and it could have been imported into Ireland by one of the many Continental scholars who sought refuge here during the 'barbarian' invasions of what is now France, at the beginning of the fifth century, which is ironic considering that Maon was himself descended of French stock.

When Cobhthach Caoilbreagh became Ard-Righ of Ireland he greatly wronged Maon. Maon was the son of Oilill Aine who was the son of Laoghaire Lorc, Cobhthach's brother and previous Ard-Righ, both of whom Cobhthach had murdered to ascend the throne.

Maon, who was then but a child, was brought into Cobhthach's presence and was there compelled to swallow a portion of his father's and grandfather's hearts, and also a mouse with her young. From the disgust he felt, the child lost his speech, and seeing him dumb, and not perceiving him to be a threat, Cobhthach let him go.

The child then set out for Feara Morc, the kingdom of South Munster, of which Scoiriath was king, and remained with him for some time, but afterwards went to France, his great-grandmother's country, where his nine guards told the king that he was heir to the throne of Ireland, and because of this he was treated with great honour, and the French king made him leader of his household guards. He became very successful, and his fame was great in Ireland, many Irishmen following him to France as a result. He remained there for a large part of his life.

But Moiriath, daughter of Scoiriath the King of Feara Morc, had conceived a violent passion for him that could not be stilled, on account of the greatness of his name, and she resolved to bring him back to Ireland.

She accordingly equipped Craiftine the harper, who was in Ireland at that time, with many rich gifts, and wrote a love-lay, in which she set forth the intensity of her passion for Maon, and to which Craiftine composed a melody.

When he arrived in France, Craiftine made his way to the king's court. In those days being of the profession of harpers was a sufficient passport to enter the presence of royalty. He found Maon there, and he played a very sweet tune on his harp and sang the love-lay which Moiriath had composed for him. So deeply stirred was Maon by the beauty and passion of the song and the grace and quality of Craiftine's harping that his speech returned to him and he broke out into praises of it.

He resolved to return to Ireland, and requested the King of France to grant him an army, so that he might regain his kingdom, which the king readily agreed to.

They landed at Loch Garman and, learning that Cobhthach was then at Dionnriogh (ancient seat of the

kings of Leinster, near Leighlinbridge, Co. Carlow), they
marched day and night and attacked his fortress, slaying
Cobhthach along with many of his nobles.

After the slaughter a druid who was in the fortress
asked one of the French who their leader was.

"The Mariner," (an Loingseach) replied the man,
meaning Maon, the captain of the fleet.

"Does the Mariner speak?" inquired the druid, who had
begun to suspect the truth.

"He speaks" (Labhraidh) said the man; and from then
onwards the name Labhraidh Loingseach clung to Maon
son of Oilill, nor was he known by any other. He then
went with Craiftine to visit Moiriath, the lady who had sent
Craiftine to France. Labhraidh married her and she was
his queen during life.

Labhraidh reigned over Ireland ten years. It was his
custom to have his hair cropped but once a year, and the
man to do this was chosen by lot, and was immediately
afterwards put to death.

The reason for this was that he had long ears like those
of a horse, and he would not have this deformity known.

Once it fell, however, that the person chosen to crop
his hair was the only son of a widow who approached the
close of her life. When she heard that the lot had fallen
on her son, she came and beseeched the king not to put
her only son to death, seeing as he was her sole offspring.
The king promised her that he would not put her son to
death, provided he kept secret what he should see, and
made it known to no one till death. The oath was taken
and, after trimming the king's hair, the young man returned
to his mother.

But by and by the secret so preyed on his mind that he
fell into a wasting sickness, and no medicine availed him.
When he had lain long in this condition, a skilful druid
came to visit him.

"It is a secret that is killing him," said the druid, "and he will never be well till he reveals it. Since he is bound not to tell his secret to a person, let him go along the road till he comes to a place where four roads meet, there turn to the right, and the first tree he shall meet on the road, let him tell his secret to that, and he shall be rid of it and recover."

So the youth did; and the first tree was a willow. He laid his lips close to the bark, and whispered his secret to it. When he did the burden of pain that was on his body vanished, and he was healed as he returned to his mother's house.

But it chanced that shortly after this the harper Craiftine's harp got broken, and he went to seek the material for a new one, and as luck would have it the first suitable tree he came to was the willow that held the king's secret.

When the harp was made and tuned, as Craiftine played upon it all who listened imagined that it sang, "Two horses ears on Labhraidh Loingseach."

As often as he played on the harp it sung the same thing. When the king heard about this, he repented of having put so many people to death on account of his ears, and openly exhibited them to his household and no longer concealed them.

Which makes a Harper

Hebrides

*Coming from the same islands as "The Harper's Pass", this cryptic tale
also holds a message. The explanations of all three harpers of the event
which shaped the rest of their lives can be interpreted in a number of
ways, but I believe that in each instance what is represented is the
harper's spiritual awakening, from which arose a desire to bring a
similar awakening to others, through the medium of music.*

On Rhum, one of the islands of the Inner Hebrides,
there is a cave which is known only to the lobster-
fishers, and to the otters. In front of it there is a wrecked
smack, partly covered with sea-pinks. From its mouth one
can see the Cuillin hills on the Isle of Skye.

One day, long ago, three galleys, each from a different
isle, put into the creek nearby; and the three crews with
their harpers met in the cave at the greying of night.

Shortly before dawn the harping ceased, and those who
were listening asked, softly but eagerly, how the harpers
had come by the itch for music.

Said one harper: "My mother was a medicine woman
who spent her days amongst the hills, looking for the
plants of healing. Her boy got the knowing from her, and
the wonder of not knowing."

Said the second harper: "I was herding a widow's one
cow in a deserted sheiling. I saw a gnarled oak tree
standing alone, and a bird's nest in one of its branches. I
climbed up to give a few worms to the little ones. The nest
was empty. A thought and a sorrow came to me."

Said the third harper: "It was a boat that came to our
creek. There was a woman in her, and she sang a strange

tune, something from another shore. It was a tune that beckoned me. My fingers will always be feeling now for that other shore."

"Which makes you a harper," said the listening ones.

"Which makes me a little child," said the harper.

Retold by Kenneth MacLeod

Thady Elliot

Ireland

The harpers of ancient Ireland were treated like royalty, they sat on the right hand of their lord, were entitled to lands and honour from him and often came from high-born families. A thousand years later, times had changed. The harp was now often learnt by those, either blind or lame, who could follow no other profession. Thady was such a man, and, like many of his contemporaries, was very fond of a drop o' the pure.

Thady came from County Meath, and it was he who taught Rose Mooney how to play the harp, and she went on to take third place at all three Granard festivals. Edward Bunting had a low opinion of his general character. Arthur O'Neill, on the other hand, was widely respected, and his memoirs give a rare insight into the life of an itinerant harper in the mid to late eighteenth century.

One Christmas Day, Thady Elliot was to play at the Roman Catholic chapel at Navan. A practical joker took Thady to a bar and promised to give him a gallon of whiskey if he would rattle up "Planxty Connor", a merry dance tune by O'Carolan, at the time of the Elevation, which Thady promised to do.

Accordingly, when Mass commenced on Christmas Day, Thady as usual played some sacred airs until the Elevation, when, for the sake of the whiskey and to be as good as his word, he lifted up "Planxty Connor". The priest, who was a good judge of music, knew the tune, but at that solemn stage of the ceremony he could not speak to Thady, so to show his disapproval he stamped violently and repeatedly where he stood at the altar, so much so that the people exclaimed in Irish, "Dhar Dhiah, thaw Soggart a dhounsa," that is, "By God, the priest is dancing." However after playing "Planxty Connor" for some time, he resumed his usual airs. When Mass was over Thady was severely reproved and dismissed.

On Thady Elliot's disgrace the priest applied to the young Arthur O'Neill to succeed him in the chapel, which he declined, not wishing to supersede Thady who had always been civil to him, but recommended Harry Fitzsimmons, a harper who had come to hear Mass in Navan. He readily accepted, borrowed O'Neill's harp, and played during the remainder of the Masses.

In the meantime, Thady, to be revenged of him, returned to his lodgings, got a long staff, and coming back to the chapel offered any one of the congregation half of the whiskey if they would tell him when Fitzsimmons was coming out. Some of them agreed to, but on the priest coming out one fellow cried, "Tage, dhar Dhiah, shin eh," (Thady, by God, there he is). With that Thady began to lay about him furiously, and made one desperate blow, which struck the chapel door; if the priest had got it he would not have said Mass for a long time.

Thady, who was as great a devil as ever lived, was so much vexed with his mistake that he went to the chapel and made a public apology for his behaviour.

The Power of the Harp

Sweden

At one time it was customary throughout Scandianvia for all nobles to be able to play the harp. If a commoner played one they were put to death.

The Nikke is a river spirit. It is described as being a monster with a human head, that dwells both in fresh and salt water. When anyone was drowned, it was said the Nikke had taken them away; and when any drowned person was found with their nose red, it was said that the Nikke had sucked them.

In the Icelandic Sagas we find Odin in the Nikke's disguise of an old man, wringing the water from his long beard as he sits on the cliffs. The Nikke bears a striking resemblance to the Scottish Kelpie, which also has a particular liking for young women. The Kelpie is sometimes called a Water Horse, just as the Nikke appears in one of its guises as half-human, half-horse. While both the Nikke and the Kelpie are commonly depicted as using trickery to catch their prey, the main difference between the two is that the Nikke is credited with great skill on the harp, while the Kelpie has no talent for music. Both are credited with the swelling of the river fords and the carrying away of unwary travellers. As recently World War One, Scottish shepherds regularly claimed to have seen the Kelpie swimming upon the surface of the lochs. Perhaps we should rename Loch Ness, Loch Kelpie.

One evening in late summer, two boys were playing beside the Ringfalla river that ran by their house.

"Beware the Nikke that lives at the bottom of the Ringfalla," their father had said. "Every summer he steals one of our people for his supper; but summer is nearly over and he has not yet claimed his victim. Be careful, for he can take many forms, all of them deceitful, and if he doesn't eat you straight away, then he will force you to be his servant at the bottom of the river."

They did not believe in the Nikke. But just as the sun was setting one of the boys let out a startled cry; floating upon the surface of the Ringfalla river he saw a pretty little boy sitting cross-legged, playing a golden harp. The boys knew this to be the Nikke and they threatened to stab him with their iron knives if he tried to attack them. The Nikke realised that what had seemed easy prey would elude him, and in a fit of rage he flung his harp onto the banks of the river, and sank into its depths in despair.

The boys retrieved the harp from where it had fallen and took it home to their father. This sensible man recognised that the harp had magic in it, and decided it was best left in the hands of a man whose soul was pure. So he took the harp to a nobleman who lived some distance away, and was rewarded with a grant of good land, away from the river.

Sir Peter, as was the custom for the nobility of that time, had been taught how to play the harp, although his playing was not of a high standard. But from the moment the first notes of this harp broke forth under his fingers, none could surpass him in quality or style. It was his beautiful playing that had first attracted his sweetheart Kerstin to him, and before long they were betrothed.

On the eve of the wedding, Kerstin was sitting in the courtyard as usual with Sir Peter, who was playing some particularly joyful tunes, when she suddenly burst into tears. He laid aside his harp and clasped her in his arms.

"Love of my heart, tell me why do you grieve so? Have I not goods and servants enough to meet your needs? Or is it that you regret having agreed to marry me?"

"I do not grieve for goods or for servants, and I certainly do not grieve because I have you, I could not wish for a more noble man. I grieve beloved because I am the last of three sisters. Both Sigrid and Astrid also found themselves good husbands, but each in turn, on their wedding day, was claimed by the Nikke of Ringfalla. My only route to meet you at the marriage grounds leads over the slippery bridge of Ringfalla. The Nikke has not claimed a victim this year, and I fear that I will share the fate of my sisters, that my fair gold hair will be stained with my blood before the day is out."

"Then I shall send my courtiers to escort you, they will protect you from harm. Twelve of them before you, and twelve upon each side, and all of their horses shall be shod with gold, so they will not stumble."

This reassured Kerstin, but she was still uneasy, and spent a restless night. The next day dawned bright and clear so that, by the time Sir Peter's courtiers came to escort her to the wedding, she had rid herself of her fears of the previous day. The little procession set off, and all went well until they reached the forest that stood between her home and the Ringfalla. There the courtiers sighted a young stag with proud, spreading horns and, without a second thought, every man of the escort rode off in hot pursuit, leaving Kerstin to continue on alone and unguarded.

Her old fears now returned as she rode through the forest, but no harm befell her there. She reined in her horse and hesitated before the slippery bridge over the Ringfalla. On the other side were the marriage grounds, and she could see Sir Peter waiting for her there, but what lay in wait for her in between? With a deep sigh she started her horse across the bridge. Just as she crossed the point where the Ringfalla flowed deepest, the water started bubbling, and a gorgeous young man rose up to his waist out of the water. But Kerstin could see below the surface of the water, and from the waist down he had the body of a horse. Her steed reared in fright at this apparition, tossing Kerstin into the river, where the Nikke swiftly clutched her and dragged her down to his lair.

"Quickly, bring me my gold harp, it hangs from my saddle," said Sir Peter to his page.

No sooner were the words out of his mouth, than it was thrust into his hands. That noble man held the gold harp in his strong arms, and with the first stroke of his fingers upon the strings, the foul Nikke rose up in the form of an old man with a long beard, and sat upon the waves and mocked him. The second time he swept his fingers across the strings, the Nikke started to feel the power of the harp and sat upon the waves and wept. With the third stroke he drew Kerstin above the waves by her snow-white arms. Sir Peter played on until the bark fell from the trees, and the foul Nikke had placed Kerstin at his side once more. Still Sir Peter played on, and in despair the Nikke swam down to the riverbed, tore Kerstin's two sisters away from their tasks, and brought them to the shore, then fled again to the quiet of his lair.

When Astrid and Sigrid had recovered, they happily accompanied their sister to her marriage rites, and to such a fine man they said. After a month of festivities Sir Peter decided it was about time he was left alone with his wife. So he escorted the two maidens back to their lovers, who had remained faithful to their trust. He then returned home, banished his faithless courtiers from his lands forever, and lived happily with Kerstin for the rest of his days.

The Fairy Harp

Wales

In Wales the fairies are called the Tylwyth Teg, and are almost identical to their Irish and European counterparts. They often test people's generosity as a way of deciding their worthiness for a gift. The mad, destructive dance that Morgan inflicts on the unfortunate bard and the others is in sharp contrast to involuntary good humour of the dance in "The Bee, The Harp, the Mouse and the Bum-clock". Although there are quite a few instances of instruments that play of their own accord, and instruments whose playing gives one an irresistible desire to dance, I am not aware of any other tale that includes both themes.

A company of fairies, who lived in the recesses of the great mountain of Cader Idris, were in the habit of going about from cottage to cottage in that part of the country to test the disposition of its inhabitants. Those who gave the Fairies an ungracious welcome were subject to bad luck for the rest of their lives; but those who were good to the folk who called on them in disguise could receive substantial favours.

Old Morgan ap Rhys was sitting one night by himself in his own chimney corner, solacing his loneliness with his pipe and some fine Llangollen ale. The heady liquor made Morgan light hearted, and he began to sing – at least he was under the impression that he was singing. His voice, however, was anything but sweet. A bard whom he had offended likened it to the yelping of a blind dog, or the lowing of a cow which has lost its way to the cowyard. His singing, however, gave Morgan himself much satisfaction, and this particular evening he was especially pleased with the harmony he was producing. The only thing which marred his contentment was the lack of an audience.

However, just as he was coming to the climax of his song, he heard a knock at the door. Delighted that here at last was someone to listen to him, Morgan sang with all the fervour he was capable of, and his top note was, in his opinion, a thing of beauty and joy. When he had finished, he called out merrily: "What is the door for but to come in by? Come in, come in, whoever you may be."

The door opened and in came three travellers, travel stained and weary looking. "Good Sir," said one of them, "we are worn and tired, but all we seek is a bite of food to put in our wallets, and then we will be on our way."

"Brensiach," said Morgan, "is that all you want? Well there, look you, is the loaf and the cheese, and the knife lies by them. You just cut however much you like. Never let it be said that Morgan ap Rhys denied bread and cheese to strangers." The travellers proceeded to help themselves, and Morgan, determined not to fail in his hospitality, sang to them while they ate, only pausing to moisten his throat with more ale whenever it became dry.

After they had eaten, the travellers said: "Good Sir, we thank you for our entertainment. Since you have been so generous we will show that we are grateful. It is in our power to grant you a wish; tell us what that wish may be."

"Well, indeed," said Morgan, "the wish of my heart is to have a harp that will play under my fingers, no matter how ill I strike it; a harp that will play only lively tunes, none of that melancholy music for me. But surely it's making fun of me you are."

Barely had he finished speaking when, to his astonishment, there on the hearth before him stood a splendid harp, and when he looked up to thank his guests, he found they had vanished. "That's the most extraordinary thing," he exclaimed, "they must have been Fairies." After calming his nerves with ale, he decided to try the instrument . As soon as his fingers touched the strings, the harp began to play a mad and capering tune.

Just then there was the sound of footsteps, and in came his wife with some friends. No sooner did they hear the strains of the harp than they began dancing, and as long as Morgan's fingers were on the strings they kept footing it like mad creatures.

The news that Morgan had come into possession of a harp with some mysterious power spread like wildfire over the whole country, and many were the visitors who came to see him and it. Every time he played it, all who heard felt compelled to dance, and could not leave off until Morgan stopped playing. Even lame people capered away, and a one legged man who visited him danced as merrily as any man with two.

One day, among the company who had come to see if the stories about the harp were true, was the bard who had made unpleasant remarks about Morgan's singing. A spitefulness stole over Morgan, and he determined to pay the bard out. So instead of stopping as usual after the dance had been going for a few minutes, he kept on playing. He played on and on until the dancers were exhausted and shouted to him to stop. He laughed until his sides ached and the tears rolled down his cheeks at the antics of his visitors, and especially at those of the overfed bard. The longer he played, the madder became the dance; the dancers spun round and round, wildly knocking over the furniture, and some of them bounded up against the roof of the cottage until their heads cracked. Morgan did not stop until the bard was unconscious and had broken both his legs, and the rest had been jolted almost to pieces. By that time his revenge was satisfied, and his sides and jaw were so tired with laughing that he had to take his fingers away from the strings.

But this was the last chance he was to have of venting

his spite. When he awoke, the next morning, the harp had disappeared and was never seen again. The Fairies were annoyed at the use to which their gift had been put, and had reclaimed it during the night.

Retold by W. Jenkyn Thomas

The Lord of the Isles

Hebrides

There has been a long tradition among Irish harpers of travelling through Scotland and the Isles. For over fifteen hundred years they have spread the fame of their harping, and played their part in Scotland's history. The renowned Irish harper Rory Dall O'Cahan rebuked King James VI of Scotland for his treachery toward Brian O'Neill, and Denis Hempson played before Bonnie Prince Charlie at Holyrood.

When Angus Og MacDonald assumed the Lordship of The Isles he also inherited a bitter feud with the MacKenzies, which had begun when his sister, Lady Margaret, who had been the first wife of Kenneth MacKenzie, had been set aside in favour of another. Angus continued this feud by using his new power to regain some lands that his father had conceded to the MacKenzies, with considerable loss to them.

Now the MacKenzies determined to repay the Lord of the Isles for their defeat. Angus had also fallen foul of a daughter of Rory Dubh MacLeod, and the two chiefs plotted his death.

At that time there was, in Inverness, an Irish harper by the name of Diarmid O'Cairbre, and the impressionable young man had become captivated by the charms of the MacKenzies' daughter. The chief summoned the harper, and promised him that if he could bring about the death of Angus Og, then he would grant him his daughter in marriage. O'Cairbre resolved to win the girl, and succeeded in attaching himself to Angus' coterie, where his harping was much admired, and he gained great trust within their ranks.

When Angus was at Inverness in 1487, on his way to attack the MacKenzies once more, O'Cairbre stole into his bedchamber and slit his throat while he slept, in the midst of his attendants. He was immediately captured by the Islesmen, who found tokens from both Mackenzie and MacLeod upon his person, and knew that it was their old enemies who had been behind the killing. They dealt mercilessly with the unfortunate harper and, after subjecting him to many tortures, he was tied between horses and torn apart. His head was hung from a pole by its throat, and his skull was later used as a drinking cup.

The Bee, the Harp, the Mouse and the Bum-clock

Ireland

The simpleton who is apparently bested in a bargain, but gets a better deal of it in the end, is a common theme in folk tales the world over. The irresistible urge to dance is similar to that in "The Fairy Harp", though in this case the urge is purely benign. The Fairy Folk were often on the lookout for cattle to add to their own herds, so the man who sells Jack these wonderful creatures is obviously one of the Good People himself.

Once there was a widow, and she had one son, called Jack. Jack and his mother owned just three cows. They lived well and happy for a long time, but at last hard times came down on them, and the crops failed, and poverty looked in at the door, and things got so sore against the poor widow that, for want of money and necessities, she made up her mind to sell one of the cows.

"Jack," she said one night, "go over in the morning to the fair and sell the branny cow."

Well and good. In the morning my brave Jack was up early, and took a stick in his fist and turned out the cow, and off to the fair he went with her, and when he came into the fair, he saw a great crowd gathered in a ring in the street. He went into the crowd to see what they were looking at, and there in the middle of them he saw a man with a wee, wee harp, a mouse, a bum-clock (cockroach), and a bee to play the harp. When the man put them down and whistled, the bee began to play the harp, and the mouse and the bum-clock stood up on their hind legs and got hold of each other and began to waltz. As soon as the harp began to play and the mouse and the bum-clock to dance, there wasn't a man or woman, or a thing in the fair, that didn't begin to dance also, and the pots and pans, and the wheels and the reels, jumped and jigged all over the town, and Jack himself and the branny cow were as bad as the next.

There was never a town in such a state before or since, and after a while the man picked up the bee, the harp, the mouse and the bum-clock, and put them into his pocket, and the men and women, Jack and the cow, the pots and pans, wheels and reels, that had hopped and jigged now stopped, and every one began to laugh as if to break its heart. Then the man turned to Jack.

"Jack," says he, "how would you like to be master of all these animals?"

"Why," says Jack, "I should like it fine."

"Well then," says the man, "how will you and me make a bargain about them?"

"I have no money," says Jack.

"But you have a fine cow," says the man, "I will give you the bee and the harp for it."

"Oh, but," says Jack, says he, "my poor mother at home is very sad and sorrowful entirely, and I have this cow to sell and lift her heart again."

"And better than this she cannot get," says the man. "For when she sees the bee play the harp, she will laugh if she never laughed in her life before."

"Well," says Jack, says he, "that will be grand."

He made the bargain. The man took the cow, and Jack started home with the bee and the harp in his pocket, and when he came home his mother welcomed him back.

"Jack," says she, "I see you have sold the cow."

"I have done that," says Jack.

"Did you do well?" says the mother.

"I did well, and very well," says Jack.

"How much did you get for her?" says the mother.

"Oh," says he, "it was not for money at all I sold her, but for something far better."

"Oh, Jack, Jack!" says she. "What have you done?"

"Just wait until you see mother," says he, "and you will soon say I have done well."

Out of his pocket he takes the bee and the harp and sets them in the middle of the floor, and whistles to them, and as soon as he did this the bee began to play the harp, and the mother she looked at them and let a big, great laugh out of her, and she and Jack began to dance, the pots and pans, the wheels and reels began to jig and dance all over the floor, and the house itself hopped about also.

When Jack picked up the bee and the harp again the dancing all stopped, and the mother laughed for a long time. But when she came to herself, she got very angry entirely with Jack, and she told him he was a silly, foolish fellow, that there was neither food nor money in the house, and now he had lost one of her good cows also.

"We must do something to live," says she. "Over to the fair you must go tomorrow morning, and take the black cow with you and sell her."

Off in the morning at an early hour brave Jack started, and never halted until he was in the fair. When he came into the fair he saw a big crowd gathered in a ring in the street. Said Jack to himself: "I wonder what are they looking at?"

Into the crowd he pushed, and saw the wee man this day again with a mouse and a bum-clock, and he put them down in the street and whistled. The mouse and the bum-clock stood up on their hind legs and got hold of each other and began to dance and jig, and as they did there wasn't a man or woman in the street who didn't begin to dance and jig also, and Jack and the black cow, and the wheels and reels, and the pots and pans, all of them were jigging and dancing all over the town, and the houses themselves were jumping and hopping about, and such a place Jack or anyone else never saw before.

When the man lifted the mouse and the bum-clock into his pocket they all stopped dancing and settled down, and everybody laughed right hearty. The man turned to Jack.

"Jack," says he, "I am glad to see you, how would you like to have these animals?"

"I should like well to have them," says Jack, says he, "only I cannot."

"Why cannot you?" says the man.

"Oh," says Jack, says he, "I have no money and my poor mother is very downhearted. She sent me to the fair to sell this cow and bring some money to lift her heart."

"Oh," says the man, says he, "if you want to lift your mother's heart I will sell you the mouse, and when you set the bee to play the harp and the mouse to dance to it, your mother will laugh if she never laughed in her life before."

"But I have no money," says Jack, says he.

"I don't mind," says the man, says he, "I will take your cow for it."

Poor Jack was so taken with the mouse and had his mind so set on it, that he thought it was a grand bargain entirely, he gave the man his cow, and took the mouse and headed for home, and when he got home his mother welcomed him.

"Jack," says she, "I see you have sold the cow."

"I did that," says Jack.

"Did you sell her well?" says the mother.

"Very well indeed," says Jack.

"How much did you get for her?" says the mother.

"I didn't get money," says he, "but I got value."

"Oh, Jack, Jack!" says she. "What do you mean?"

"I will soon show you that mother," says he, taking the mouse out of his pocket and the harp and the bee and settling all on the floor, and when he whistled the bee began to play, and the mouse got up on its hind legs and began to dance and jig, and the mother gave such a hearty laugh as she never laughed in her life before. To dancing and jigging herself and Jack fell, and the pots and pans, and the wheels and reels, began to dance and jig all over the floor, and the house jigged also. When they were tired of this Jack lifted the mouse, harp and bee and put them in his pocket, and his mother she laughed for a long time.

But when she got over that, she got very downhearted and very angry entirely with Jack.

"Oh, Jack," says she, "you are a stupid, good for nothing fellow. We have neither money nor meat in the house and here you have gone and lost two of my good cows, and I have only one left now. Tomorrow morning," she says, "you must be up early and take this cow to the fair and sell her. See to get something to lift my heart up."

"I will do that," says Jack.

Bright and early in the morning brave Jack set out with the spotty cow, and never halted until he reached the fair. When he came to the fair, he saw a big crowd gathered in a ring in the street.

"I wonder what are they looking at?" said Jack to himself.

Into the crowd he shoved and pushed, and saw the wee man this day again with a bum-clock, and he put it down in the street and whistled, the bum-clock stood up on its hind legs and began to jig, and as it did there wasn't a man or woman in the street who didn't begin to jig also, and Jack and the spotty cow were amongst the worst, and the wheels and reels, and the pots and pans, all of them were dancing and jigging all around the town, and the houses themselves were jumping and hopping about also,

As soon as the harp began to play... there wasn't a man or woman, or a thing in the fair, that didn't begin to dance also...

and such a place no one ever saw before.

When the wee man lifted the bum-clock into his pocket, they all stopped jigging and settled down, and everyone laughed right long and loudly. The man turned to Jack.

"Jack, my brave lad," says he, "you will never be right fixed until you have this bum-clock, for it is a fancy thing to have."

"But I have no money," says Jack.

"You have a cow," says the man, "and that is as good as money."

"But," says Jack, "I have a poor widowed mother at home who is very downhearted, and she has sent me to the fair to sell our last cow to get some money to lift her heat up."

"Ah, Jack," says the man, "this bum-clock is the very thing to make her heart rise with joy."

"Well, that is surely true," says Jack, "and I think I will make a swap with you."

The wee man took the cow, and Jack took the bum-clock and started off for home, and when he got home his mother welcomed him.

"Jack," she says, "I see you have sold the cow."

"I have done that," says Jack.

"Did you sell her well then?" says the mother.

"I sold her very well indeed, mother," says Jack.

"How much did you get for her?" she says.

"I didn't get money," says he, "but I got value and more."

"Oh, Jack!" says she. "Whatever have you done?"

"I will show you that mother," says he. And he took the bum-clock out of his pocket and the mouse and the harp and the bee and settled all on the floor, and when he whistled the bee began to play the harp, and the mouse and the bum-clock got up on their hind legs, took hold of each other and began to waltz and to jig, and the mother gave a roaring laugh that shook the walls. Both Jack and herself to dancing and jigging fell, and the pots and pans, and the wheels and reels, began to dance and jig all over the floor, and the house was hopping and jigging too.

When Jack lifted up the animals and put them in his pocket, everything stopped, and the mother laughed for a good while. But after a while, when she came to herself, and saw what Jack had done, and how they were now without either money or food, or a cow, she got very, very angry at Jack, and scolded him hard, and then sat down and began to cry.

Poor Jack, when he looked at himself, confessed that he was a stupid fool entirely.

"And what," says he, "shall I now do for my poor mother?"

He went out along the road, thinking and thinking, and he met a wee woman who said:

"Good morrow to you Jack," says she, "how is it you are not trying for the King of Ireland's daughter?"

"What do you mean?" says Jack.

Says she, "Didn't you hear what the whole world has heard? That the King of Ireland has a daughter who hasn't laughed for seven years, and he has promised to give her in marriage, and the kingdom along with her, to any man who will take three laughs out of her."

"If that is so," says Jack, says he, "it is not here I should be."

Back to the house he went, and gathers together the bee, the harp, the mouse and the bum-clock, and putting them into his pocket he bade his mother goodbye, and told her it wouldn't be long till she got news from him, and off he hurries.

When he reached the castle, there was a ring of spikes around it, and men's heads on nearly every spike there.

"Whose heads are these?" Jack asked one of the King's soldiers.

"Any man that comes here trying to win the King's daughter and fails to make her laugh three times, loses his head and has it stuck on a spike. Those are the heads of the men that failed," says he.

"A mighty big crowd," says Jack, says he. Then Jack sent word to tell the King's daughter and the King that there was a new man that had come to win her.

In a very little time the King and the King's daughter and the King's court all came out and sat themselves down in front of the castle, and ordered Jack to be brought in until he should have his trial. Jack, before he went, took out of his pocket the bee, the harp, the mouse and the bum-clock, and he gave the harp to the bee, and he tied a string to the bee, the mouse and the bum-clock, and took the end of the string himself, and marched into the castle yard before all the court, with his animals coming along on a string behind him.

When the Queen and King and the court and princes saw poor ragged Jack with his bee, his mouse and bum-clock hopping behind him on a string, they set up one roar of laughter that was long and loud enough, and when the King's daughter herself lifted her head and looked to see what they were laughing at, and saw Jack and his paraphernalia, she opened her mouth and she let out of her such a laugh as was never heard before.

Then Jack dropped a low courtesy and said: "Thank you, my lady; I have one of the three parts of you won."

Then he drew up his animals in a circle, and began to whistle, the bee started playing on the harp, and the mouse and the bum-clock stood up on their hind legs, bowed to each other, and began to dance and to jig for all they were worth, and the King and the Queen and all the King's court were all dancing and jigging, and the pots and pans, the wheels and reels, were all jumping about, and the castle was hopping all over the grounds with its turrets wobbling about. Now the King's daughter when she saw this, opened her mouth again, and let out of her a laugh twice louder than she let before, and Jack, in the middle of his jigging, drops another courtesy.

"Thank you, my lady," says he, he says, "I now have two parts of you won."

Jack and his menagerie went on playing and dancing, but Jack could not get the third laugh out of the King's daughter, and the poor fellow saw his big head in danger of going on the spike. Then the brave mouse came to Jack's help and wheeled around upon its heel, and as it did so its tail swiped into the bum-clock's mouth, and the bum-clock began to cough, and cough, and cough. When the King's daughter saw this she opened her mouth again, and she let out the loudest and proudest and merriest laugh that was ever heard before or since.

"Thank you, my lady," says Jack, dropping another courtesy, "I have all of you won."

Then when Jack stopped his menagerie, the King took himself and the menagerie within the castle. He was washed and combed, and dressed in a suit of silk and satin, with all kinds of gold and silver ornaments, and then he was led before the King's daughter. True enough, she confessed that a handsomer and finer fellow than Jack she had never seen, and was very willing to be his wife.

Jack sent for his poor old mother and brought her to the wedding, which lasted nine days and nine nights, every night better than the last. All the lords, ladies and gentry of Ireland were at the wedding. I was at it too, and got brogues, broth, and slippers of bread, and came jigging home on my head.

Retold by Seumas MacManus

The O'Neill

The Milesians get their name from the sons of Milidh, whose people drove out the Tuatha De Danann. Their descendants used to consider themselves to be the only true Irish, and Lord Kenmare's ancestor was one of them. It was once fashionable among the Anglo-Irish to be able to claim a family tie with the Milesians.

Around 1753 the principal proprietor of Killarney, its lakes and the surrounding countryside, was Lord Kenmare. The first of his family to settle on those lands had married a daughter of the great O'Sullivan of Beara, and his ancestral relationship with the native Irish was a matter of considerable pride to this Anglo-Irish Lord.

So Lord Kenmare took it upon himself to entertain, at Christmas time, every Milesian that could be found that bore the name of an Irish chieftain, including the O'Neills, O'Briens, MacCarthys, O'Donoghues, O'Driscolls, O'Connors, O'Donovans, O'Sullivans, O'Connor Kerry, MacNamaras, O'Keeffes, O'Meaghers, O'Learys, O'Callaghans, O'Connells, O'Mahonys, MacGillacuddys, and some others of the Milesian race that my memory at present will not enable me to mention.

At the feast there was one or more of every Milesian name present, except for the noble family of O'Neill. Lord Kenmare observed this omission and, remembering Hugh O'Neill's league with the great Munster chieftains, mentioned his disappointment to one of his guests, Murtagh MacOwen O'Sullivan.

"Och," he replied, "upon my honour I can soon fill up that gap for you, as I have at my house right now a young man from the north by the name of Arthur O'Neill, who is blind and plays very well on the harp for his years, and I have it from his own lips that he has a good enough claim to represent the O'Neills on this occasion, or any other."

"Well, send for him then," says Lord Kenmare.

The young harper Arthur O'Neill was sent for, and was ushered into the Great Hall, where he was seated amongst the other Milesians before dinner. Hundreds of questions were asked him concerning his descent, and it was only after giving them satisfactory answers that he was dubbed and deemed a true O'Neill.

When dinner was announced, very nearly two hundred of the O's and Mac's took their seats, while O'Neill, being blind, was left to grope for a vacancy near the foot of the table. Such a noise of cutting, carving, roaring, laughing, shaking hands, and raucous language, you would hear only at a gathering of friends who only see each other once a year.

While dinner was going on, just about every gentleman present made a point of speaking to the harper, and to congratulate him on his illustrious ancestry. But when Lord Kenmare came to speak to him, that good man said: "O'Neill, you should be sitting at the head of the table, your ancestors were the original Milesians of this kingdom."

"Oh, my lord," replied the harper boldly, "it doesn't matter where an O'Neill sits; for let it be known that at whatever part of the table I am, then it should be considered the head of it."

The Harper's Gratuity

This tale is chock full of familiar themes. It is said that on certain occasions the Fairies need a human at their festivities, usually to entertain them or to play sports with them, and on these occasions their reward, if it is given in coin, later turns to dust or dried leaves and is blown away on the wind. If, however, the gift of healing or second sight is granted, then this remains in that family until they prove themselves no longer worthy of it. The Fairies knowledge of human affairs is shown by their addressing Sion by name, without him telling it. The splendid mansion, where none had been known to exist before, has a Scandinavian counterpart. When the Trolls, who live in the hills, wish to have a banquet, they raise the top of a selected hill upon red pillars, and entice humans to join them, where they are trapped, and are forced to serve the Trolls for at least seven years.

Sion Rhobert was a harper living at Hafod Elwy in Denbighshire. One evening he went to Llechwedd Llyfin, to a fine party, and it was late before the lads and lasses separated. At last he was allowed to wend his way homeward, and he started walking over the bare mountain. As he came near a lake called Lyn-dau-ychain he saw on its verge a splendid palace, brightly illuminated. He was very surprised, because he had been that way many times before without observing a dwelling house of any kind.

When he came near a splendid servant invited him to enter. Sion was ushered into a great room, lit by thousands of candles and sumptuously furnished. His cup was filled with sparkling wine, after drinking which Sion felt convinced that he was, without a shadow of a doubt, the best harper that the world had ever seen. The guests surrounded him

The palace had vanished, and the gold and silver in his hat
had turned into withered leaves.

and asked him to play. Sion consented, and the company began to dance very spiritedly.

When the first dance was over one of the guests took Sion's hat and collected money for him, bringing it back filled with gold and silver. After this Sion kept on playing, and the company continued to dance until the dawn of day, when one by one the guests disappeared, and Sion was left alone. Seeing a couch, he laid himself down, and was soon fast asleep. He did not wake until midday, and then he found himself lying on the heather. The palace had vanished, and the gold and silver in his hat had turned into withered leaves.

Retold by W. Jenkyn Thomas

Prince Edward in the Holy Land

England

It seems likely that Robert would have been more than just a confidante of Edward. Whatever the case may be, at least this harper discharged his friendship with honour, unlike his countryman who was bound to the Lord of the Isles. Some accounts have Edward's harper rushing into the tent to find that the assassin was already dead, then picking up a wooden stool and belabouring the corpse with it.

When Prince Edward of England set off for the Holy Land in 1270, on the last great crusade, he took with him his harper, Robert. They landed at Acre in May of the following year, and during the coming seasons it was Edward's custom to have Robert near him at all times, to lift his spirits above the corruption and petty bickering that he encountered.

Despite the weakness of his forces, Edward successfully negotiated a truce of ten years, ten months, ten days, ten hours, with Baibars, the Sultan. Baibars needed the truce to give himself time to secure the lands he already held, but knowing that Edward intended to return at the head of a larger crusade he approached the tribe of Assassins, who were known mercenary killers, and paid them to kill Edward as soon as possible. With this intention a number of the Assassins attached themselves to Edward's camp following, disguised as native Christians.

In June of 1272, Edward was camped at Ptolemais. He lay in his apartments before his evening meal. Normally he would dine with Robert, but he had been detained elsewhere in the camp. As usual, a servant brought his food and tasted it before retiring. The fine food after a gruelling day made Edward relaxed, so he did not notice that the servant who came to claim his dishes was not the same one who had brought them.

The Assassin drew his flame-edged poisoned dagger and lunged for Edward's heart, but Edward was still quick enough to realise his intent and threw himself to one side, while the blade sliced a furrow across his ribs. The two men grappled with each other across the floor. During the struggle Robert strode into the tent and, realising his master's life was at stake, quickly plunged his sword through the traitor's body.

When news reached Baibars of the failure of his plan, he sent word to Edward congratulating him on his lucky escape. Edward was seriously ill for some months as a result of the poison, and returned to England soon afterwards. He learnt that his father had died during his return voyage, and that he was now King. And Robert, the king's harper, was rewarded handsomely for saving his life.

Retold by Brenda Girvin

How the Mystic Harp saved Moy

Scotland

Fairies were counted to have both good and evil ones amongst their number. This tale combines bad Fairies with the very early common belief that music was endowed with powers of magic, with the harp in particular being held in high esteem. The early missionaries adopted the instrument and its beliefs into their own rituals, thus endowing themselves with a spurious magical ability.

Near Loch Katrine there stands a romantic forest called Glenfinlas. It was in this forest that the highland chieftains Ronald and Moy were hunting, when a strange adventure befell them.

They had been riding for three summer days through brake and dell, when they came one evening across a lonely hut which stood in the depths of the wood. They were so pleased with the hut that they thought they would rest there for a while. So Ronald made a fire and cooked some venison, while Moy played upon the Mystic Harp, which had been given him by a hermit.

When Ronald put the crackling venison upon the table, Moy laid his harp aside. He was pleased with the fare.

"We lack nothing here," he said, as he filled his cup and quaffed the wine.

Ronald, however, was not so easily contented.

"I would," he answered, "that the fairest of our mountain lassies could be here to wait upon us."

The words were scarcely out of his mouth when a beautiful girl appeared in the doorway. She was dressed in green, and Ronald was enchanted with her. When she began to dance he rose to dance with her, while Moy took up his harp to play upon it.

Ronald danced after the Green Lady from corner to
corner, as she swayed to and fro before him and looked
back over her shoulder, laughing and tossing her long
golden hair. Artfully, she brought him to the door of the
hut.

"Follow me," she coaxed.

Ronald danced after her. The happy music which the
charmed harp played now became sad and sorrowful. At
once Moy sprang to his feet and threw the harp aside.

"Stop! Stop!" he warned Ronald. "I hear groans, I see
tears. Danger threatens you if you follow the Green Lady
of the Glen." Ronald laughed, whistled to his hounds,
and, without another word, plunged into the darkness.
Moy buried his head in his hands.

An hour later the hounds returned and crouched about
him. They all waited until midnight. Still no Ronald.
Then a strange thing happened. The harp, which lay
forgotten on the table, though untouched, began to sing.
Its tune was mournful.

The hounds shivered and howled. Moy looked up as
the door opened, and there entered another Fairy of the
Glen, who was also dressed in green. Her hair was wet
with dew, and she was even more beautiful than the Fairy
who had enticed Ronald from the hut. She had come to
claim Moy.

She did not dance or sing. She appealed to the chieftain's
kind heart.

"I have lost my way, kind stranger," she began. "I dare
not venture through the woods alone, for it is dark. For
pity's sake, guide a wanderer across the haunted brake,
for I must reach my father's castle of Glengyle before day
dawns."

The hut was filled with music from the harp. It was a
thousand times more sad, a thousand times more tearful

than it had ever been before. Moy turned his head away.

"You refuse to help a lost wanderer? Shame on your knighthood!"

Still Moy turned away from the wicked Fairy. He seized up his harp and then his fingers played the wildest witch notes. They were loud, and high, and strange.

As he played, the Green Lady grew taller and taller. She grew until her head knocked against the roof. Then the roof of the hut was swept away, and she was thrown out into the Northern skies. Down into the hut the rain beat and the hail rattled. When at last the storm abated and day came, Moy went out into the forest to look for Ronald. Alas! he could not find his wilful friend, though he combed every inch of the Glen of the Green Ladies, as that dark glen is called until this day.

Retold by Brenda Girvin

The Tsaritsa Harpist

Russia

The harp in Russia was known as a gusla or gusli, and the harpist as a guslyar. Although few musical scores exist in which it is specifically mentioned, there are a great many pictures in which it is shown with other instruments, and we can assume from these that it was used to complement their sounds.

The flourishing court music of Russia was severly inhibited in the late 12th century when Bishop Cyril Turovsky severely proscribed all the arts. Above all he castigated music, which he regarded as an emanation of Hell. Those musicians who had formerly enjoyed the patronage of the courts now had to choose between becoming street entertainers, or retiring to the provinces. This story must predate that action, or the Tsaritsa would have been seen as a servant of Hell herself.

A representative of the epic tradition of the late 13th and 14th centuries was the bard Riabinin who displayed its essential characteristics; the use of ancient poetic modes, a severe style, and a sung recitation accompanied by the gusli. Which is very similar to the Gaelic tradition.

I n Russia there once lived a Tsar and Tsaritsa, who had lived together for some time and were happy. The Tsar had long cherished a desire to visit the Holy Land, and eventually that desire became irresistible. So he issued orders to his ministers, bade farewell to his wife, and set out on his long journey.

At last he reached that distant land where Christ is said to have been crucified. In that country at that time an Accursed King was the ruler, and he mistrusted all foreigners, because he thought they would steal the holy relics. So when this King saw the Tsar he bade him be seized and lodged in the dungeon. There were many tortures in that dungeon for him. At night he must sit in chains, and in the morning the Accursed King put a horse-collar on him, and made him pull a plough through the scorching heat of the day until the evening. This was the torment in which the Tsar lived for three whole years, and he had no idea how he could tear himself away or send news of himself to his Tsaritsa. One day another prisoner who was being set free promised to deliver a message to the Tsaritsa. So the Tsar wrote begging her to sell all his possessions and come and redeem him from his misfortune.

When the Tsaritsa read the letter she said to herself: "How can I redeem the Tsar? If I go myself, the Accursed King will take me to himself as a wife. If I send one of the ministers, I can place no reliance on him." So what did she decide to do? Despairing of any other solution, she cut off her long red hair, went and disguised herself as a wandering musician, took up her gusli, and set out on her own road without telling anybody.

She arrived at the courtyard of the Accursed King's palace and began to play the gusli more finely than had been heard in that country for years. The King was entranced, and summoned the guslyar into his palace.

"Hail guslyar, from what land have you come? From what kingdom?" asked the King.

"I journey through many lands, yet call none my home, but can bring joy to men's hearts and am able to feed myself," replied the guslyar.

"Stay with me one day, and another day, and a third and I will reward you generously," said the King.

So the guslyar stayed on and played for an entire day in front of the King, and he could never hear enough of her. "What music!" he told the guslyar. "It has driven away all my weariness and my grief. What reward can I offer you?"

"Just this your Majesty, give me one of your prisoners as a companion on the road. I wish to go to foreign kingdoms, and have no one with whom I can exchange a friendly word."

"Certainly, select whom you will," said the King, and he led the guslyar into the dungeons.

The guslyar looked carefully at the prisoners, selected the Tsar, who was now weak and thin, and they went out on the road together, with the Tsar as her bondsman. As they were journeying toward their own kingdom the Tsar said: "Let me go good man, for I am no simple prisoner, but the Tsar himself. I will pay you a ransom of as much as you wish; I will grudge you neither money nor service."

"Go with God," said the guslyar, "I have no need of your money or your services."

"Well then, come with me as my guest."

"When the time shall come, I will be there."

So they parted as friends, and each set out on their own way. The Tsaritsa went by a faster and more dangerous route and reached home before her husband. There, she took off her guslyar's dress and arrayed herself like an empress.

Not long afterwards cries rung out and the attendants came running up to the palace, in a frenzy of delight. The Tsar had come home. The Tsaritsa ran out to meet him, but he was cool towards her, then turning to his ministers he said: "Look gentlemen, what a wife mine is! Now she flings herself on my neck, but whilst I rotted in prison and begged her to redeem me, she did nothing. Of what was she thinking if she so forgot her liege husband?"

And the ministers answered the Tsar: "Your Majesty, on the day the Tsaritsa received your letter she vanished no one knows where, she has been away all this time and has only just recently appeared in the palace."

To which the Tsar thundered: "My ministers, judge my unfaithful wife according to justice and to truth. Where has she been? Why did she not try to redeem me? You

*The Tsaritsa arrayed herself as the guslyar, went into the
courtyard and began to play...*

would not have seen your Tsar again but for the playing of a young guslyar, and if he wished it I would not grudge giving him half my kingdom."

In the meantime the Tsaritsa arrayed herself as the guslyar, went into the courtyard and began to play her gusli. The Tsar heard and ran to meet the musician, whom he took by the hand and led into the palace, where he said to his court: "This is the guslyar who rescued me from my confinement." The guslyar then flung off his outer garment, and the Tzar recognised the Tsaritsa, and was humble. She redeemed him, and in his joy the Tzar held a feast which lasted seven whole days.

St Brendan and the Harper

Ireland

*St Brendan came from a 'pagan' family, his father was named Findlug
in honour of the pagan God Lugh, but despite this he was at the
forefront of Christianity's assault on paganism and this tale reflects
that. Most harpers of his day would have played at least some tunes that
had pagan associations, which would have been distasteful to a devout
man of the cloth. If we take the harp as representative of paganism and
its traditions, and the angel as the messenger of the new faith, then what
we have here is a symbolic rendering of the saint's preference for his new
God over the Old Ones.*

One Easter Day, seven years before his death, St Brendan
celebrated mass at Clonfert. After the ceremony the
monks went to their refectory, where there was a student
playing on the harp, and they gave him their blessings, on
account of his mastery.

"I should be delighted," said the student, "if I could see
Brendan, that I might play him three tunes."

"He would not let you into his presence," said the monks,
"for Brendan has been seven years without smiling and
without hearing any of the music of the world; for he has
two balls of wax with a thread joining them on the book
before him, and whenever he hears music he puts the
balls in his ears."

"I shall go, nevertheless, to play for him," said the student.

He went to Brendan's chambers with his harp tuned
and ready.

"Open, good Brendan, I would like to come and play
my harp for you," said the student.

"Play outside, I have no wish to hear it," replied Brendan.

"If you would not think it troublesome," said the student, "I would be grateful if you allowed me to play inside."

Brendan reluctantly agreed and, reaching for his balls of wax, invited him inside. The student took his harp from his back and prepared to play.

"There is no point in letting me play for you if you don't take the wax out of your ears," said the student.

"So be it then," said Brendan, removing the wax. The student played him three of his finest tunes, after which Brendan gave him a blessing and put the balls back into his ears, as he did not wish to listen any more.

"Why do you not listen to the music?" asked the student. "Is it because you think it unworthy?"

"Not for that reason," said Brendan, "but this. One day when I was in this church, seven years ago to this very day, when Mass was over and the priest had gone to the refectory, I was left there alone, and a great longing for my Lord seized me. A trembling and a terror came upon me. I saw a shining bird at the window and it glided down to sit on the altar. I was unable to look directly at it because of the rays that surrounded it, like those of the sun. 'A blessing upon you, and do you bless me priest,' it said. 'May God bless you,' I replied, 'but who are you?' 'I am the angel Michael,' it replied, 'and I have come to bless you and make music for you from our Lord.' The bird set its beak on the side of its wing, and I was listening to it for a full day, when I found myself alone once more."

Brendan scraped his stylus across the neck of the student's harp. "Do you think this sweet, student?" said Brendan. "I give my word before God, that after hearing the music of that bird, no music of the world seems any sweeter to me, than does the screech of this stylus across the neck of your harp."

A Harp of Fishbones

This is a modern tale, but blended into it are threads of history and lore from different eras. Kira is a contemporary symbol of spiritual awakening, just as some of the other symbolism used represents an earlier awareness. We need more love in this world, and music has the power to bring it forth.

K ira was a poor peasant girl. Her parents had died soon after she was born, so she had been placed in the care of a childless couple who ran a small farm in the next valley. She worked hard from dawn to dusk, and her evening meal consisted of little more than scraps, which was all her foster parents were able to provide.

One night as Kira lay in her bed crying because the biting of the fleas kept her awake, she heard a strange music whispering in the still night air. She climbed out of her bedroom window and walked around to try and locate the sound, or even which direction it came from. But it seemed to be a part of the air around her, so she climbed to the top of a nearby hill to try and trace its source, and all the while the eerie music was wrapping her in its spell.

From the hilltop, Kira saw a light shining in the forbidden valley, a glen which all the local people avoided, especially after dark, and the air seemed to shimmer as the music swept in waves up the hillside towards her. She felt herself being drawn .towards the light and was soon amongst the trees which filled the valley floor. Gnarled and bent they stood, and Kira instinctively knew them to be ancient. Now the music stopped, and through the trunks of the trees she saw a clearing ahead, and walked towards it.

As she stepped into the glade she became aware that

Through the trunks of the trees she saw a clearing ahead...

this was no natural clearing. It was perfectly circular, and around the grove stood twelve large upright stones, with strange symbols carved upon each of them, and before each stone stood a different tree, and the trees seemed to draw strength from the stones, for they were fine and strong. Before her stood the reed, the elder, the birch, and the rowan, to her left there stood the holly, the hazel, the vine, and the ivy, while to her right there stood the oak, the willow, the alder, and the ash. While directly before her in the centre of the grove stood a large hawthorn in full bloom, and at its base a long flat stone was laid, upon which stood the first harp that Kira had ever seen. It appeared to be made of bone, and it was so finely carved that the figures seemed to run together as if in a dance, and so bleached that the moon reflecting on its surface was the light which had guided her to it. Automatically Kira reached out to take hold of the harp, and as she did so she heard a voice which seemed to come from the hawthorn itself.

"Patience girl, your time has not yet come. Sit for a while, and listen to the story of this harp."

"Many generations ago a fleet of ships came across the seas to the land you now live in. Thirteen brothers led them, but they could not agree on how to divide this land amongst themselves, so they split into groups and they and their followers waged war on each other for many years until only two of the brothers, Coll and Uath, and their remaining followers were left alive, and these two agreed that they alone should meet in single combat on board a ship anchored off the shore. So they fought to the death, and after a hard battle Coll slew his elder brother and threw the body over the side of the ship, where it was swallowed whole by a large, savage fish. It was then that Coll realised that he was the only one of his family left alive. In a fit of remorse he dived overboard, wrestled with, and finally slew the fish. When he returned to shore he had the fish cut open and Uath's body removed. His people feasted on the fish and Coll himself made this harp of its bones, stringing it with strands of his brother's hair. Uath's remains they laid beneath the stone before you, with his other brothers gathered round, while Coll left the harp here as a gift to the future. He had seen a vision and knew that there would come a time when there would be no music to stir men's souls, to lift their spirits high, when greed and lust would dominate men. So we have waited, and protected this harp for many centuries until the day of its need, and that day is close at hand. You have been chosen by the Old Ones to bring light back into this world, but you will not be ready until three years after your moon-cycles have begun and, provided you have not lain with any man, you may then claim the harp and carry it forth into many lands, bringing the return of peace and love with you. We trust in your resolve for the coming seasons. Now rest before your journey home."

When Kira awoke again she was back in her room, but not once did she think that her experience could have been a dream. She treasured every moment of its memory, and knew her life would no longer be the same. She saw her world through new eyes, saw into men's hearts and minds, and what she saw was distasteful. The years rolled on and her moon-cycles began. She was now considered a woman, but no man succeeded in tempting her into his embrace, though they tried many times.

Kira awoke one fine May morning and knew that her time had finally come. The sun was drawing the dew off the new mown hay, the birds were singing in the fields, a light breeze ruffled the tops of the trees, and in a patch of sunlight at the foot of her bed lay the harp of fishbones she had last seen so many years earlier.

She clasped it to her, as if embracing the lover she had

never known, and drew her fingers gently across the strings. It responded with a song of joy. She played it for her step-parents, and their faces lost their care-worn looks, and they wondered at their happiness.

That night she carried the harp to the local tavern, a place where no decent woman went alone. No sooner was she inside the doors than she was grabbed from behind, and the harp was torn from her fingers. Kira was terrified. She was lifted up and sat on the bar, where they could get a better look at her, and then they started to argue over who should have her first.

With all the commotion the harp had been kicked into a corner of the room, and now it began to pour forth its own song, softly at first but slowly getting louder, like the breeze rising into a gale. It forced itself on the attentions of everyone in the tavern, and all were held spellbound. Kira went and took up the harp, and she played songs of life and songs of passing, songs of love and songs of healing, and all of those that heard and felt the power of the harp, were touched, and lost their malice.

Then she filled a small pack with a few belongings and set off into the unknown world, banishing greed and lust and misery wherever she went, and leaving peace and love in their stead. Her task is not yet finished, so still she travels, and there are many who have not yet heard her song, and have retained their greedy, wicked ways, but their time, too, will come.

Select Bibliography

Armstrong, Robert Bruce, *The Irish and Highland Harps* (David Douglas, 1904)

Croker, Thomas Crofton, *Fairy Legends and Traditions of the South of Ireland Vols I–III* (John Murray, 1825)

Dunbar, Sir A. H., *Scottish Kings*

Flood, William H. Grattan, *The Story of the Harp* (Walter Scott Ltd, 1905)

Fox, Charlotte Milligan, *Annals of the Irish Harpers* (Smith, Elder & Co, 1911)

Furlong, Alice, *Tales of Fairy Folks, Queens and Heroes* (Browne & Nolan)

Gantz, Jeffrey (Trans), *Early Irish Myths and Sagas* (Penguin Classics, 1981)

Graves, Robert, *The White Goddess* (Faber & Faber, 1962)

Gray, Elizabeth A. (Ed), *The Second Battle of Mag Tuired* (Irish Texts Society, 1982)

Gregory, Donald, *History of the Western Highlands and Isles of Scotland* (William Tait, 1836)

Gunn, John, *An Historical Enquiry Respecting the Performance of the harp in the Highlands of Scotland* (Constable, 1807)

Jackson, Kenneth Hurlstone, *A Celtic Miscellany* (Penguin Classics, 1971)

Keating, Geoffrey, *The History of Ireland Vols I–IV* (Irish Texts Society, 1901–14)

Keightley, Thomas, *The Fairy Mythology* (H. G. Bohn, 1850)

MacLeod, Kenneth, *The Road to the Isles* (Grant & Murray, 1933)

MacManus, Seumas, *Donegal Fairy Stories* (Dover Publications)

MacNeill, Nigel, *The Literature of the Highlands* (John Noble, 1892)

Magnus, Leonard A., *Russian Fairy Tales*

Morris, William, *The Story of Sigurd the Volsung*

O'Curry, Eugene, *Manners & Customs of the Ancient Irish Vols I–III* (Williams & Norgate, 1873)

O'Neill, Captain Francis, *Irish Minstrels & Musicians* (Mercier Press, 1987)

Panum, Hortense, *The Stringed Instruments of the Middle Ages* (William Reeves, 1990)

Rimmer, Joan, *The Irish Harp*, (Mercier Press, 1977)

Rolleston, T. W., *Myths and Legends of the Celtic Race* (Constable, 1987)

Sanger, Keith & Kinnaird, Alison, *Tree of Strings, or Crann Nan Teud* (Kinmor Music, 1992)

Thomas, W. Jenkyn, *The Welsh Fairy Book*

Walsh, John R. & Bradley, Thomas, *A History of the Irish Church 400–700AD* (Columba Press, 1991)

Wyse, Rev. John, *A Thousand Years, or The Missionary Centres of the Middle Ages* (Society for Promoting Christian Knowledge, c1930)

The Most Unpretending of Places

A History of Dundonald, County Down
Peter Carr
Pbk, 256pp, illustrated, £7.95

"Sparkles with compelling detail... one of the most impressive local histories available for any locality on this island, north or south."
Linenhall Review

"One word could suffice to describe this book, magnificent! ...I cannot praise it too highly. Well illustrated with photographs, studiously annotated without over-loading the text, a questioning of sources, a good index and the courage to express opinions of a controversial nature. This is what local history is all about."   *Irish News*

Farewell to the Hammer

A Shankill Boyhood
John Young Simms
Pbk, 144pp, illustrated, £4.95

A fascinating story of growing up, amidst horses, trams, cobbles and pig's feet, in the Hammer district of Belfast's Shankill Road at the height of the Great Depression.

"Each tale swells in the mind, like grain in water, until the reader finds it necessary to pause, savour its taste, and go back over it again before moving the short distance to the next..."   *Sam McAughtry*

Gape Row

Agnes Romilly White's classic comedy
Pbk, 200pp, £4.95

Can Jinanna escape the poorhouse? Will young Johnny Darragh jilt Ann? Will Mary get saddled with the awful Andy John McCready? Or will Happy Bill, the wayside preacher, nip in first and win them all for God?

A boisterous, rich, nostalgic book which immerses the reader in the cheerful chaos of everyday life in a small Irish village on the eve of the First World War.

"Captures the spirit of early twentieth century rural Ulster better than any painter of photographer could."   *Sunday News*

"masterly... the dialogue goes to one's head like wine."   *The Observer*

Available from bookshops, or directly from the publishers.
If ordering, please add £1 for postage and packaging.